The Constitution of
The State of Alabama:
As Adopted in 1901

Bootblack Budget Books
Copyright 2018 ©
ISBN-13: 978-1985318977
ISBN-10: 1985318970

Contents:

Preamble – Page 36

Article I: Declaration of Rights – Page 37

Section 1. Equality and Rights of Men

Section 2. People Source of Power

Section 3. Religious Freedom

Section 4. Freedom of Speech and Press

Section 5. Unreasonable Search and Seizure; Search Warrants

Section 6. Rights of Persons in Criminal Prosecutions Generally; Self-Incrimination; Due Process of Law; Right to Speedy, Public Trial; Change of Venue

Section 7. Accusation, Arrest and Detention; Punishment Limited to Laws Established Prior to Offense

Section 8. Proceeding Against Person by Information; Grand Jury Not Required in Misdemeanor Cases

Section 9. Double Jeopardy; Discharge of Juries from Cases

Section 10. Right to Prosecute Civil Cause

Section 11. Right to Trial by Jury

Section 12. Prosecutions for Libel or for Publication of Papers Investigating Official Conduct of Public Officers

Section 13. Courts to Be Open; Remedies for All Injuries; Impartiality of Justice

Section 14. State Not to Be Made Defendant

Section 15. Excessive Fines; Cruel or Unusual Punishment

Section 16. Right to Bail; Excessive Bail

Section 17. Suspension of Habeas Corpus

Section 18. Treason Against the State

Section 19. Bills of Attainder of Treason by Legislature Prohibited; Conviction Not to Work Corruption of Blood or Forfeiture of Estate

Section 20. Imprisonment for Debts

Section 21. Suspension of Laws

Section 22. Ex Post Facto Laws; Impairment of Obligations of Contracts; Irrevocable or Exclusive Grants of Special Privileges or Immunities

Section 23. Eminent Domain

Section 24. Navigable Waters Declared Free Public Highways; Taxes, Tolls, Etc., for Use of Shores or Wharves

Section 25. Right to Peaceably Assemble and Petition for Redress of Grievances, Etc.

Section 26. Right to Bear Arms

Section 27. Standing Army; Military Subordinate to Civil Power

Section 28. Quartering of Soldiers in Houses

Section 29. Titles of Nobility, Hereditary Distinction, Etc.; Restriction on Appointments to Office

Section 30. Immigration, Emigration and Exile

Section 31. Residence Not Forfeited by Temporary Absence from State

Section 32. Slavery Prohibited; Involuntary Servitude

Section 33. Protection of Suffrage

Section 34. Property Rights of Aliens

Section 35. Objective of Government

Section 36. Construction of Declaration of Rights

Article II: State and County Boundaries – Page 46

Section 37. State boundaries defined.

Section 38. County boundaries ratified and confirmed.

Section 39. Arrangement and designation of county boundaries; new counties.

Section 40. Minimum distance of county boundaries from courthouse.

Section 41. Removal of courthouse or county site.

Article III: Distribution of Powers of Government -- Page 48

Section 42. Legislative, executive and judicial departments established.

Section 43. Separation of powers.

Article IV: Legislative Department – Page 49

Section 44. Composition of legislature.

Section 45. Style of laws; division of laws; laws restricted to one subject; amendment or revival of laws by title only.

Section 46. Election and terms of office of senators and representatives; vacancies in office.

Section 47. Qualifications of senators and representatives.

Section 48. Time and place of meetings of legislature; maximum length of sessions.

Section 49. Compensation of members of legislature.

Section 50. Number of senators and representatives; apportionment of legislators.

Section 51. Election of president pro tem. of senate and speaker of house of representatives; temporary president and speaker; officers of each house; each house judge of election, returns and qualifications of members.

Section 52. Quorum in each house.

Section 53. Rules of proceedings of both houses; punishment for contempt or disorderly behavior; enforcement of process; protection of members from violence, bribes, etc.; expulsion of members.

Section 54. Expulsion for corruption bar to further service in legislature; punishment for contempt or disorderly behavior not bar to indictment for same offense.

Section 55. Journal of proceedings of each house.

Section 56. Immunity of legislators.

Section 57. Doors of each house to be open; exceptions; restrictions on admittance to floor.

Section 58. Adjournment or change of place of sitting by one house without consent of other house.

Section 59. Appointment of legislators to other offices during terms for which elected.

Section 60. Conviction of certain crimes bar to eligibility for legislature and to holding state office of trust or profit.

Section 61. Laws to be passed by bills; restrictions on amendments to bills.

Section 62. Referral of bills to standing committees.

Section 63. Number of readings for bills; recordation of votes on bills; majority vote required for passage of bills.

Section 64. Procedure for amendment of bills; adoption of reports of committees of conference.

Section 65. Lotteries and gift enterprises prohibited.

Section 66. Signature of bills by presiding officer of each house; reading of bills at length may be dispensed with.

Section 67. Number, duties and compensation of officers and employees of each house.

Section 68. Extra compensation not to be granted public officer, employee, contractor, etc., after service rendered or contract made; increase or decrease of compensation of officers during term of office.

Section 69. Stationery, printing, fuel, etc., to be furnished by lowest responsible bidder; conflicts of interest.

Section 70. Revenue bills to originate in House of Representatives; preparation of general revenue bill; amendments to revenue bills by Senate; time limit for passage of revenue bills.

Section 71. Restrictions on general appropriation bill.

Section 72. Payment of money out of state treasury; publication of annual statement of receipts and expenditures.

Section 73. Appropriations to charitable or educational institutions not under absolute control of state.

Section 74. Authorization of investment of trust funds by executors, trustees, etc., in bonds or stock of private corporations prohibited.

Section 75. Change of venue in civil and criminal cases.

Section 76. Restrictions on legislation at special sessions; duration of special sessions.

Section 77. State office for inspection or measuring of merchandise, commodities, etc., prohibited.

Section 78. Legislation to change seat of government of state.

Section 79. Bribery — Solicitation, acceptance, etc., of bribes by legislators.

Section 80. Same — Offer, gift, etc., of money, etc., to executive or judicial officers or members of legislature to influence official acts.

Section 81. Offense of corrupt solicitation to be defined by law.

Section 82. Disclosure of personal or private interest in bills, etc., by legislators.

Section 83. Voting in elections by legislature.

Section 84. Adoption of laws to provide for arbitration between parties.

Section 85. Periodic revision and promulgation of laws.

Section 86. Suppression of dueling.

Section 87. Deductions from salaries or compensation of public officers for neglect of duty.

Section 88. Counties to provide for maintenance of the poor.

Section 89. Municipalities not to pass laws in conflict with general laws of state.

Section 90. Acquisition of foreign territory; rights and privileges of inhabitants of acquired territory.

Section 91. Exemption from taxation of state, county, municipal, cemetery and certain religious, educational and charitable property.

Section 92. Rules and regulations to ascertain value of property exempted from sale under legal process.

Section 93. State not to engage in internal improvements or lend money or credit for same; state interest in private or corporate enterprises prohibited.

Section 94. Municipalities not to grant public money or lend credit to private persons or corporations.

Section 95. Impairing obligation of contracts; revival of barred rights or remedies; removal of cause of action or defense to suit after commencement of suit.

Section 96. Uniformity of laws regulating court costs and charges and fees, commissions and allowances of public officers.

Section 97. Payment of salary of deceased officer after date of death.

Section 98. Payments or grants to retiring officers.

Section 99. Restrictions on donation or sale of state lands to private corporations or individuals; grant of easements to railroad, telephone and telegraph companies.

Section 100. Obligations and liabilities of corporations, etc., held or owned by state, counties or municipalities.

Section 101. Lobbying in legislature by state or county officials.

Section 102. Miscegenation laws.

Section 103. Regulation, etc., of common carriers, partnerships, associations, trusts, monopolies and combinations of capital.

Section 104. Special, private or local laws — Prohibited in certain
cases.

Section 105. Same Prohibited in cases provided for by general law; exception as to time of holding courts; partial repeal of general laws.

Section 106. Same Publication or posting of notice of intent to apply therefor within county or counties affected prior to introduction of bill.

Section 107. Same Notice required by section 106 prerequisite to repeal or amendment.

Section 108. Suspension of general laws for benefit of individuals or private corporations; exemption of individuals or private corporations from operation of general laws.

Section 109. General laws for protection of local and private interests.

Section 110. "General law," "local law" and "special or private law" defined.

Section 111. Amendment of bill introduced as general law so as to become special, private or local law on passage.

Article V: Executive Department -- Page 73

Section 112. Composition; officers enumerated.

Section 113. Supreme executive power vested in Governor.

Section 114. Governor, lieutenant governor, attorney-general, state auditor, secretary of state, state treasurer, superintendent of education and commissioner of agriculture and industries— How elected; when election held.

Section 115. Same Returns of election transmitted to speaker of house of representatives; opening and publication of election returns; duties of speaker and legislature ministerial in opening and publication of votes; person having highest number

Section 116. Same Term of office; officers not eligible to succeed selves; governor not eligible for other state office or senate of United States during term or within one year thereafter.

Section 117. Qualifications of governor and lieutenant governor; lieutenant governor ex officio president of senate.

Section 118. Compensation and residency requirements for governor, lieutenant governor, attorney-general, state auditor, secretary of state, state treasurer, superintendent of education and commissioner of agriculture and industries.

Section 119. Increase in salary of governor at session of legislature following ratification of Constitution.

Section 120. Governor to faithfully execute laws.

Section 121. Governor may require reports from officers of executive department and officers and managers of state institutions; false reports or failure to file reports constitutes impeachable offense.

Section 122. Governor authorized to convene legislature on extraordinary occasions; proclamation of governor to state matters on which action necessary.

Section 123. Reports and information to be given legislature by governor; presentation of budget to legislature.

Section 124. Authority of governor to remit fines and forfeitures and grant reprieves, paroles, commutations of sentence and pardons; board of pardons; report by governor to legislature; pardons in cases of felonies and offenses involving moral turpitud

Section 125. Presentation of bills to governor for signature; veto power of governor; procedure for passage of bill after veto by governor; effect of failure of governor to sign bill.

Section 126. Authority of governor to veto items in appropriation bills.

Section 127. Succession to office of governor; filling of vacancy when offices of governor and lieutenant governor both vacant; procedure when governor or successor impeached, absent from state, disabled, etc.; failure of governor-elect, lieutenant gove

Section 128. Procedure when governor or acting governor appears to be of unsound mind.

Section 129. Compensation of acting governor.

Section 130. Holding office in addition to that of governor.

Section 131. Military powers of governor.

Section 132. Qualifications of attorney-general, state auditor, secretary of state, state treasurer, superintendent of education and commissioner of agriculture and industries.

Section 133. Great seal of state.

Section 134. Duties of secretary of state generally.

Section 135. Issuance and execution of grants and commissions.

Section 136. Vacancy in office or unsoundness of mind of attorney-general, state auditor, secretary of state, state treasurer, superintendent of education or commissioner of agriculture and industries.

Section 137. Duties generally and restrictions on receipt of fees, etc., by attorney-general, state auditor, secretary of state, state treasurer, superintendent of education and commissioner of agriculture and industries; annual report by state treasure

Section 138. Election and term of office of sheriffs; sheriff not eligible to succeed self; impeachment of sheriff; effect of impeachment of sheriff.

Article VI: Judicial Department -- Page 86

Section 139. Vesting of judicial power; minimum standards for establishment of courts of general jurisdiction in counties.

Section 140. Jurisdiction of supreme court generally; power of supreme court to issue certain remedial and original writs.

Section 141. Place of holding supreme court.

Section 142. Division of state into circuits; residency requirements for circuit judges.

Section 143. Jurisdiction of circuit courts.

Section 144. When and where circuit courts to be held; circuit judges may hold court for each other; power of circuit judges to issue writs of injunction returnable to courts of chancery.

Section 145. Authority to establish courts of chancery; division of state into chancery divisions; districts within chancery divisions; residency requirements for chancellor.

Section 146. When and where chancery courts to be held; chancellors may hold court for each other.

Section 147. Certain counties need not be included in circuit or chancery divisions; minimum number of counties in circuit or chancery divisions.

Section 148. Legislature may confer jurisdiction of circuit and chancery court on either court; consolidation of courts in counties having two or more courts of record.

Section 149. Legislature may establish court of probate in each county; powers generally of probate courts.

Section 150. Compensation and restrictions on holding other offices for supreme court justices, chancellors and judges of circuit and other courts of record, except probate judges.

Section 151. Composition of supreme court.

Section 152. Election of supreme court justices, judges of circuit courts, judges of probate courts and chancellors.

Section 153. Election or appointment of judges of inferior courts.

Section 154. Qualifications of chancellors and judges of courts of record.

Section 155. Terms of office of supreme court justices, chancellors and judges of circuit and probate courts.

Section 156. Time of holding election for supreme court justices; staggered terms of office for supreme court justices.

Section 157. Judicial officers conservators of the peace.

Section 158. Vacancies in office of supreme court justices, elected judges and chancellors.

Section 159. Initial appointment or election of judges or chancellors for newly created circuits or chancery divisions.

Section 160. Procedure when judge or chancellor incompetent to try, hear or render judgment in case.

Section 161. Failure of judges or chancellors to attend regular terms of court.

Section 162. Judges of courts of record not to practice law.

Section 163. Appointment, qualifications, terms of office and compensation of registers in chancery; fees of registers of chancery to be uniform throughout state.

Section 164. Appointment and term of office of clerk of supreme court; selection of clerks of inferior courts.

Section 165. Election and term of office of clerks of circuit courts; clerk may serve as register in chancery; filling of vacancies in office of clerk.

Section 166. Removal of clerk of supreme court and registers in chancery.

Section 167. Election, qualifications, terms of office and compensation of circuit solicitors; appointment or election of county solicitors.

Section 168. Election of justices of the peace and constables; jurisdiction of justices of the peace; fees of justices of the peace and constables; appeals from justices of the peace; terms of office of justices of the peace and notaries public; appoint

Section 169. Exclusion of persons from courtroom in cases of rape and assault with intent to ravish.

Section 170. Style of all processes.

Section 171. Authority of legislature to abolish courts when function conferred upon some other court.

Section 172. Terms of office of incumbents not abridged.

Article VII: Impeachments – Page 98

Section 173. Governor, lieutenant-governor, attorney-general, state auditor, secretary of state, state treasurer, superintendent of education, commissioner of agriculture and industries and justices of supreme court.

Section 174. Chancellors, judges of circuit and probate courts, judges of courts from which appeal may be taken directly to supreme court, solicitors and sheriffs.

Section 175. Clerks of circuit courts, courts of like jurisdiction and criminal courts, tax collectors, tax assessors, judges of inferior courts, coroners, justices of the peace, notaries public, constables and county and municipal officers.

Section 176. Limitation on impeachment penalties; accused person liable to indictment and punishment.

Article VIII: Suffrage and Elections -- Page 101

Section 177. Age and citizenship qualifications of electors.

Section 178. Residency, registration and poll tax requirements for electors.

Section 179. Method of voting.

Section 180. Persons qualified to register as electors Prior to December 20, 1902.

Section 181. Same After January 1, 1903.

Section 182. Certain persons disqualified from registering and voting.

Section 183. Qualifications as elector required to participate in primary elections, party conventions, mass meetings or other methods of political party action.

Section 184. Applicability of article as to elections held after 1902 general election.

Section 185. Oath or affirmation when vote challenged; false oath or affirmation constitutes perjury.

Section 186. Legislature to provide for registration procedure after January 1, 1903; procedure for registration prior to January 1, 1903.

Section 187. County board of registrars to furnish list of registered voters to judges of probate by February 1, 1903; judges of probate to file list with secretary of state by March 1, 1903; term for which registration valid; certificate of registratio

Section 188. Certain information to be furnished prior to registration.

Section 189. Testimony may be required of any person other than defendant in trials of contested elections, proceedings to investigate elections and criminal prosecutions under election laws; immunity from prosecution due to testimony given.

Section 190. Duty of Legislature to pass laws regulating elections, primary elections and purging of registration lists.

Section 191. Protection against evils of intoxicating liquors at elections.

Section 192. Electors immune from arrest going to, attending and returning from elections.

Section 193. Returns of elections for certain officials to be made to secretary of state.

Section 194. Poll tax Amount; maximum age for payment; when due and payable; when delinquent; returns of collections to be separate from other collections.

Section 195. Same Payment of tax of another; advance of money for payment in order to influence vote.

Section 196. Severability of article.

Article IX: Representation -- Page 115

Section 197. Ratio of senators to representatives.

Section 198. Maximum number of members of House of Representatives; apportionment of house based on decennial census of United States.

Section 199. Duty of Legislature to fix number of representatives and apportion them among counties following each decennial census; each county entitled to at least one representative.

Section 200. Duty of Legislature to fix number of senators and divide state into senatorial districts; equality of senatorial districts; senatorial districts not to be changed until next apportioning session; division of counties between senatorial dist

Section 201. State may provide for enumeration of inhabitants for purpose of apportionment of representatives and senators.

Section 202. Initial apportionment of house of representatives.

Section 203. Initial apportionment of senatorial districts.

Article X: Exemptions – Page 120

Section 204. Personal property of value of one thousand dollars exempt from sale, execution or other process of court issued for collection of debt.

Section 205. Homestead not exceeding eighty acres or city, town or village lot not exceeding two thousand dollars in value exempt from sale, execution or other process of court issued for collection of debt; exception as to mortgages.

Section 206. Homestead of family exempt from payments of debt after death of owner during minority of children.

Section 207. Laborers' liens and mechanics' liens not barred by sections 204 and 205.

Section 208. Homestead exempt upon death of owner, leaving widow, but no children.

Section 209. Property rights of females; property of wife not liable for debts, etc., of husband.

Section 210. Waiver of right of exemption.

Article XI: Taxation -- Page 123

Section 211. Property taxes to be assessed in exact proportion to value of property.

Section 212. Power to levy taxes not to be delegated.

Section 213. Creation of state debt after ratification of Constitution; temporary loans; refunding bonds for existing indebtedness.

Section 214. Limitation on state property tax rate.

Section 215. Limitation on county property tax rates; special county taxes for public buildings, bridges and roads.

Section 216. Limitation on property tax rates of municipal corporations.

Section 217. Property of private corporations, associations and individuals to be taxed at same rate; exception as to religious, educational and charitable property.

Section 218. Counties and municipal corporations exempt from payment of charges payable from state treasury.

Section 219. Estate taxes.

Article XII: Corporations -- Page 128

Article Municipal Corporations

Section 220. Consent of municipal corporation prerequisite to use of public property for public utility or private enterprise purposes.

Section 221. Payment of state license tax, etc., not to excuse payment of other privilege and license taxes.

Section 222. Issuance of bonds by counties, municipal corporations, districts and other political subdivisions of counties.

Section 223. Limitation on assessments for public improvements by municipal corporations.

Section 224. Limitation on county indebtedness.

Section 225. Indebtedness of municipal corporations Limitation; exception as to Sheffield and Tuscumbia.

Section 226. Same Municipal corporations whose present indebtedness exceeds constitutional limitation; exception as to Sheffield and Tuscumbia.

Section 227. Liability of public utilities in municipal corporations for damages to abutting property owners.

Section 228. Maximum term of public utility franchises in cities and towns having population of six thousand or more.

Article Private Corporations

Section 229. Special laws conferring corporate powers prohibited; general law as to grant or amendment of corporate charters; corporation franchise taxes to be paid; exemption of benevolent, educational or religious corporations from franchise taxes.

Section 230. Cancellation of certain corporate charters.

Section 231. Limitation on remitting forfeiture of corporate charters.

Section 232. Foreign corporations doing business in state.

Section 233. Corporations restricted to business authorized by charter.

Section 234. Restrictions on issuance of corporate stock and bonds.

Section 235. Taking of property for public use by municipal and other corporations.

Section 236. Security for dues from private corporations; liability of stockholders.

Section 237. Issuance of preferred stock by corporations.

Section 238. Authority of legislature to revoke charters of incorporation.

Section 239. Telegraph and telephone companies.

Section 240. Corporations may sue and be sued like natural persons.

Section 241. "Corporation" defined.

Article Railroads and Canals

Section 242. When railroads and canals deemed public highways; railroad and canal companies; common carriers; rights of railroad companies generally.

Section 243. Regulation of railroad companies vested in legislature.

Section 244. Giving free passes or discount tickets to members of Legislature or officers exercising judicial functions.

Section 245. Railroad companies not to give rebates or bonuses in nature thereof; deceiving or misleading public as to rates.

Section 246. Acceptance of article prerequisite to benefits of future legislation.

Article XIII: Banks and Banking -- Page 139

Section 247. Authority of Legislature restricted.

Section 248. Banking laws to be general; specie basis; authority of banks to issue bills to circulate as money.

Section 249. Bills or notes issued as money redeemable in gold or silver; laws not to sanction suspension of specie payments.

Section 250. Preference of certain creditors in case of insolvency of bank.

Section 251. Termination of business.

Section 252. Maximum rate of interest.

Section 253. State and political subdivisions thereof not to be stockholders in banks or lend credit thereto.

Section 254. Examination of banks by public officers; semiannual reports by banks.

Section 255. Applicability of article.

Article XIV: Education -- Page 142

Section 256. Duty of legislature to establish and maintain public school system; apportionment of public school fund; separate schools for white and colored children.

Section 257. Principal from sale, etc., of school property to be preserved; disposition of income therefrom.

Section 258. Property donated or appropriated for educational purposes and estates of persons dying without will or heirs to be applied to maintenance of public schools.

Section 259. Use of poll taxes for support of public schools.

Section 260. Certain income to be applied to support and maintenance of public schools; special annual tax for schools; maximum annual levy on taxable property; priority for payment of bonded indebtedness of state.

Section 261. Percentage of school funds for teachers' salaries.

Section 262. Supervision of public schools vested in superintendent of education.

Section 263. School funds not to be used for support of sectarian or denominational schools.

Section 264. Board of trustees of state university.

Section 265. Annual payment of interest on funds of University of Alabama; authority to abolish military system at university.

Section 266. Board of trustees of Alabama Polytechnic Institute.

Section 267. Change of location of Alabama Polytechnic Institute, Alabama Schools for the Deaf and Blind or Alabama

Girls Industrial School.

Section 268. Provision for taking school census.

Section 269. Special county school taxes.

Section 270. Applicability of article to Mobile county.

Article XV: Militia -- Page 149

Section 271. Composition of militia; organizing, arming and disciplining militia; naval militia may be organized.

Section 272. Conformance with regulations governing armies of United States.

Section 273. Election or appointment of company and regimental officers.

Section 274. Volunteer organizations.

Section 275. Immunity of members from arrest while attending, going to or returning from musters, parades and elections.

Section 276. Appointment and terms of office of general officers; staffs of governor, generals and regimental and battalion commanders.

Section 277. Safe keeping of arms, ammunition, military records, etc.

Section 278. Officers and men not entitled to compensation when not in active service.

Article XVI: Oath of Office -- Page 151

Section 279. Required of members of legislature and executive and judicial officers; form; administration.

Article XVII: Miscellaneous Provisions -- Page 152

Section 280. Holding state and federal office at same time; holding two state offices at same time.

Section 281. Compensation of civil officers not to be increased or diminished during term for which elected or appointed.

Section 282. Duty of legislature to enact laws to effectuate Constitution.

Section 283. Validation of certain acts relating to bonded debt of state; governor authorized to act thereunder.

Article XVIII Mode of Amending the Constitution – Page 154

Section 284. Manner of proposing amendments; submission of amendments to electors; election on amendments; proclamation of result of election; basis of representation in legislature not to be changed by amendment.

Section 285. Election ballots; affirmative vote of majority of electors voting required for passage.

Section 286. Manner of calling convention for purpose of altering or amending Constitution; repeal of act or resolution calling convention; jurisdiction and power of convention not restricted.

Section 287. Votes by legislature on proposed amendments or bills or resolutions calling conventions; acts or resolutions proposing amendments or calling conventions not to be submitted to governor for approval.

35

Schedule – Page 157

Constitution of the State of Alabama,
as adopted by
The Constitutional Convention, September 3, 1901,
and in effect November 28, 1901.

Preamble:

We, the people of the State of Alabama, in order to establish justice, insure domestic tranquility and secure the blessings of liberty to ourselves and our posterity, invoking the favor and guidance of Almighty God, do ordain and establish the following Constitution and form of government for the State of Alabama:

Article I: Declaration of Rights

That the great, general, and essential principles of liberty and free government may be recognized and established, we declare:

Section 1. Equality and Rights of Men

That all men are equally free and independent; that they are endowed by their Creator with certain inalienable rights; that among these are life, liberty and the pursuit of happiness.

Section 2. People Source of Power

That all political power is inherent in the people, and all free governments are founded on their authority, and instituted for their benefit; and that, therefore, they have at all times an inalienable and indefeasible right to change their form of government in such manner as they may deem expedient.

Section 3. Religious Freedom

That no religion shall be established by law; that no preference shall be given by law to any religious sect, society, denomination or mode of worship; that no one shall be compelled by law to attend any place of worship; nor to pay any tithes, taxes or other rate for building or repairing any place of worship, or for maintaining any minister or ministry; that no religious test shall be required as a qualification to any office or public trust under this State; and that the civil rights, privileges and capacities of any citizen shall not be in any manner affected by his religious principles.

Section 4. Freedom of Speech and Press

That no law shall ever be passed to curtail or restrain the liberty of speech or of the press; and any person may speak, write and publish his sentiments on all subjects, being responsible for the abuse of that liberty.

Section 5. Unreasonable Search and Seizure; Search Warrants

That the people shall be secure in their persons, houses, papers and possessions from unreasonable seizure or searches, and that no warrants shall issue to search any place or to seize any person or thing without probable cause, supported by oath or affirmation.

Section 6. Rights of Persons in Criminal Prosecutions Generally; Self-Incrimination; Due Process of Law; Right to Speedy, Public Trial; Change of Venue

That in all criminal prosecutions, the accused has a right to be heard by himself and counsel or either; to demand the nature and cause of the accusation; and to have a copy thereof; to be confronted by the witnesses against him; to have compulsory process for obtaining witnesses in his favor; to testify in all cases, in his own behalf, if he elects so to do; and, in all prosecutions by indictment, a speedy, public trial, by an impartial jury of the county or district in which the offense was committed; and he shall not be compelled to give evidence against himself, nor be deprived of life, liberty or property, except by due process of law; but the Legislature may, by a general law, provide for a change of venue at the instance of the defendant in all prosecutions by indictment, and such change of venue on application of the defendant, may be heard and determined without the personal presence of the defendant so applying therefor; provided, that at the time of the application for the change of venue, the defendant is imprisoned in jail or some legal place of confinement.

Section 7. Accusation, Arrest and Detention; Punishment Limited to Laws Established Prior to Offense

That no person shall be accused or arrested, or detained except in cases ascertained by law, and according to the form which the same has prescribed; and no person shall be punished but by virtue of a law established and promulgated prior to the offense and legally applied.

Section 8. Proceeding Against Person by Information; Grand Jury Not Required in Misdemeanor Cases

That no person shall, for any indictable offense, be proceeded against criminally, by information, except in cases arising in the militia and volunteer forces when in actual service, or when assembled under arms as a military organization, or, by leave of the court, for misfeasance, misdemeanor, extortion and oppression in office, otherwise than is provided in the Constitution; provided, that in cases of misdemeanor, the Legislature may by law dispense with a Grand Jury and authorize such prosecutions and proceedings before Justices of the Peace or such other inferior courts as may be by law established.

Section 9. Double Jeopardy; Discharge of Juries from Cases

That no person shall, for the same offense, be twice put in jeopardy of life or limb; but courts may, for reasons fixed by law, discharge juries from the consideration of any case, and no person shall gain an advantage by reason of such discharge of the jury.

Section 10. Right to Prosecute Civil Cause

That no person shall be barred from prosecuting or defending before any tribunal in this State, by himself or counsel, any civil cause to which he is a party.

Section 11. Right to Trial by Jury

That the right of trial by jury shall remain inviolate.

Section 12. Prosecutions for Libel or for Publication of Papers Investigating Official Conduct of Public Officers

That in all prosecutions for libel or for the publication of papers investigating the official conduct of officers or men in public capacity, or when the matter published is proper for public information, the truth thereof may be given in evidence; and that in all indictments for libel, the jury shall have the right to determine the law and the facts under the direction of the court.

Section 13. Courts to Be Open; Remedies for All Injuries; Impartiality of Justice

That all courts shall be open; and that every person, for any injury done him, in his lands, goods, person or reputation, shall have a remedy by due process of law; and right and justice shall be administered without sale, denial or delay.

Section 14. State Not to Be Made Defendant

That the State of Alabama shall never be made a defendant in any court of law or equity.

Section 15. Excessive Fines; Cruel or Unusual Punishment

That excessive fines shall not be imposed, nor cruel or unusual punishment inflicted.

Section 16. Right to Bail; Excessive Bail

That all persons shall, before conviction, be bailable by sufficient sureties, except for capital offenses, when the proof is evident or the presumption great; and that excessive bail shall not in any

case be required.
Section 17. Suspension of Habeas Corpus

That the privilege of the writ of habeas corpus shall not be suspended by the authorities of this State.

Section 18. Treason Against the State

That treason against the State shall consist only in levying war against it, or adhering to its enemies, giving them aid and comfort; and that no person shall be convicted of treason, except on the testimony of two witnesses to the same overt act, or his own confession in open court.

Section 19. Bills of Attainder of Treason by Legislature Prohibited; Conviction Not to Work Corruption of Blood or Forfeiture of Estate

That no person shall be attainted of treason by the Legislature; and no conviction shall work corruption of blood or forfeiture of estate.

Section 20. Imprisonment for Debts

That no person shall be imprisoned for debt.

Section 21. Suspension of Laws

That no power of suspending laws shall be exercised except by the Legislature.

Section 22. Ex Post Facto Laws; Impairment of Obligations of Contracts; Irrevocable or Exclusive Grants of Special Privileges or Immunities

That no ex post facto law, nor any law, impairing the obligations of contracts, or making any irrevocable or exclusive grants of special privileges or immunities, shall be passed by the

Legislature; and every grant or franchise, privilege or immunity, shall forever remain subject to revocation, alteration or amendment.

Section 23. Eminent Domain

That the exercise of the right of eminent domain shall never be abridged nor so construed as to prevent the Legislature from taking the property and franchises of incorporated companies, and subjecting them to public use in the same manner in which the property and franchises of individuals are taken and subjected; but private property shall not be taken for, or applied to, public use, unless just compensation be first made therefor; nor shall private property be taken for private use, or for the use of corporations, other than municipal, without the consent of the owner; provided, however, the Legislature may by law secure to persons or corporations the right of way over the lands of other persons or corporations, and by general laws provide for and regulate the exercise by persons and corporations of the rights herein reserved; but just compensation shall, in all cases, be first made to the owner; and, provided, that the right of eminent domain shall not be so construed as to allow taxation or forced subscription for the benefit of railroads or any other kind of corporations, other than municipal, or for the benefit of any individual or association.

Section 24. Navigable Waters Declared Free Public Highways; Taxes, Tolls, Etc., for Use of Shores or Wharves

That all navigable waters shall remain forever public highways, free to the citizens of the State and the United States, without tax, impost or toll; and that no tax, toll, impost or wharfage shall be demanded or received from the owner of any merchandise or commodity for the use of the shores or any wharf erected on the shores, or in or over the waters, of any navigable stream, unless the same be expressly authorized by law.

Section 25. Right to Peaceably Assemble and Petition for Redress of Grievances, Etc.

That the citizens have a right, in a peaceable manner, to assemble together for the common good, and to apply to those invested with the power of government for redress or grievances or other purposes, by petition, address or remonstrance.

Section 26. Right to Bear Arms

That every citizen has a right to bear arms in defense of himself and the State.

Section 27. Standing Army; Military Subordinate to Civil Power

That no standing army shall be kept up without the consent of the Legislature, and, in that case, no appropriation for its support shall be made for a longer term than one year; and the military shall, in all cases, and at all times, be in strict subordination to the civil power.

Section 28. Quartering of Soldiers in Houses

That no soldier shall, in time of peace, be quartered in any house without the consent of the owner; nor, in time of war, but in a manner to be prescribed by law.

Section 29. Titles of Nobility, Hereditary Distinction, Etc.; Restriction on Appointments to Office

That no title of nobility or hereditary distinction, privilege, honor or emolument shall ever be granted or conferred in this State; and that no office shall be created, the appointment to which shall be for a longer time than during good behavior.

Section 30. Immigration, Emigration and Exile

That immigration shall be encouraged; emigration shall not be prohibited, and no citizen shall be exiled.

Section 31. Residence Not Forfeited by Temporary Absence from State

That temporary absence from the State shall not cause a forfeiture of residence once obtained.

Section 32. Slavery Prohibited; Involuntary Servitude

That no form of slavery shall exist in this State; and there shall not be any involuntary servitude, otherwise than for the punishment of crime, of which the party shall have been duly convicted.

Section 33. Protection of Suffrage

The privilege of suffrage shall be protected by laws regulating elections, and prohibiting, under adequate penalties, all undue influences from power, bribery, tumult or other improper conduct.

Section 34. Property Rights of Aliens

Foreigners who are, or may hereafter become, bona fide residents of this State, shall enjoy the same rights in respect to the possession, enjoyment and inheritance of property as native born citizens.

Section 35. Objective of Government

That the sole object and only legitimate end of government is to protect the citizen in the enjoyment of life, liberty and property, and when the government assumes other functions it is usurpation and oppression.

Section 36. Construction of Declaration of Rights

That this enumeration of certain rights shall not impair or deny others retained by the people; and, to guard against any encroachments on the rights herein retained, we declare that everything in this Declaration of Rights is excepted out of the general powers of government, and shall forever remain inviolate.

Article II: State and County Boundaries

Section 37. State boundaries defined.

The boundaries of this State are established and declared to be as follows, that is to say: Beginning at the point where the thirty-first degree of north latitude crosses the Perdido river; thence east, to the western boundary line of the State of Georgia; thence along said line to the southern boundary line of the State of Tennessee; thence west, along the southern boundary line of the State of Tennessee, crossing the Tennessee river, and on to the second intersection of said river by said line; thence up said river to the mouth of Big Bear creek; thence by a direct line to the northwest corner of Washington county, in this State, as originally formed; thence southwardly, along the line of the State of Mississippi, to the Gulf of Mexico; thence eastwardly, including all islands within six leagues of the shore, to the Perdido river; thence up the said river to the beginning; provided, that the limits and jurisdiction of this State shall extend to and include any other land and territory hereafter acquired, by contract or agreement with other States or otherwise, although such land and territory are not included within the boundaries hereinbefore designated.

Section 38. County boundaries ratified and confirmed.

The boundaries of the several counties of this State, as they now exist, are hereby ratified and confirmed.

Section 39. Arrangement and designation of county boundaries; new counties.

The Legislature may, by a vote of two-thirds of each House thereof, arrange and designate boundaries for the several counties of this State, which boundaries shall not be altered, except by a like vote; but no new county shall be formed hereafter of less extent than six hundred square miles, and no existing county shall be reduced to less than six hundred square miles; and no new county shall be formed unless it shall contain a sufficient number of inhabitants to entitle it to one Representative under the ratio of representation existing at the time of its formation, and leave the county or counties from which it is taken with the required number of inhabitants to entitle such county or counties, each, to separate representation; provided, that out of the counties of Henry, Dale, and Geneva a new county of less than six hundred square miles may be formed under the provisions of this article, so as to leave said counties of Henry, Dale, and Geneva with not less than five hundred square miles each.

Section 40. Minimum distance of county boundaries from courthouse.

No county line shall be altered or changed, or in the event of the creation of new counties shall be established, so as to run within seven miles of the county courthouse of any old county.

Section 41. Removal of courthouse or county site.

No courthouse or county site shall be removed except by a majority vote of the qualified electors of said county, voting at an election held for such purpose, and when an election has once been held no other election shall be held for such purpose until the expiration of four years; provided, that the county site of Shelby county shall remain at Columbiana, unless removed by a vote of the people, as provided for in an act entitled, "An act to provide for the permanent location of the county site of Shelby county, Alabama, by a vote of the qualified electors of said county," approved the 9th day of February, 1899, and the act amendatory thereof, approved the 20th day of February, 1899, or by an election held under the provisions of this article.

Article III: Distribution of Powers of Government

Section 42. Legislative, executive and judicial departments established.

The powers of the government of the State of Alabama shall be divided into three distinct departments, each of which shall be confided to a separate body of magistracy, to wit: Those which are legislative, to one; those which are executive, to another; and those which are judicial, to another.

Section 43. Separation of powers.

In the government of this State, except in the instances in this Constitution hereinafter expressly directed or permitted, the legislative department shall never exercise the executive and judicial powers, or either of them; the executive shall never exercise the legislative and judicial powers, or either of them; the judicial shall never exercise the legislative and executive powers, or either of them; to the end that it may be a government of laws and not of men.

Article IV: Legislative Department

Section 44. Composition of legislature.

The legislative power of this State shall be vested in a Legislature, which shall consist of a Senate and a House of Representatives.

Section 45. Style of laws; division of laws; laws restricted to one subject; amendment or revival of laws by title only.

The style of the laws of this State shall be: "Be it enacted by the Legislature of Alabama," which need not be repeated, but the act shall be divided into sections for convenience, according to substance, and the sections designated merely by figures. Each law shall contain but one subject, which shall be clearly expressed in its title, except general appropriation bills, general revenue bills, and bills adopting a code, digest, or revision of statutes; and no law shall be revived, amended, or the provisions thereof extended or conferred, by reference to its title only; but so much thereof as is revived, amended, extended, or conferred, shall be re-enacted and published at length.

Section 46. Election and terms of office of senators and representatives; vacancies in office.

Senators and Representatives shall be elected by the qualified electors on the first Tuesday after the first Monday in November unless the legislature shall change the time of holding elections and in every fourth year thereafter. The terms of office of the Senators and Representatives shall commence on the day after the general election at which they are elected, and expire on the day after the general election held in the fourth year after their election, except as otherwise provided in this Constitution. At the general election in the year nineteen hundred and two all the Representatives, together with the Senators for the even numbered districts and for the Thirty-fifth district, shall be elected. The terms of those Senators who represent the odd numbered districts under the law in force prior to the ratification of this Constitution, are hereby extended until the day after the general election in the year nineteen hundred and six; and until the expiration of his term as hereinbefore extended, each such Senator shall represent the district established by this Constitution, bearing the number corresponding with that for which he was elected. In the year nineteen hundred and six, and in every fourth year thereafter, all the Senators and Representatives shall be elected. Whenever a vacancy shall occur in either House the Governor shall issue a writ of election to fill such vacancy for the remainder of the term.

Section 47. Qualifications of senators and representatives.

Senators shall be at least twenty-five years of age, and Representatives twenty-one years of age at the time of their election. They shall have been citizens and residents of this State for three years and residents of their respective counties or districts for one year next before their election, if such county or district shall have been so long established; but if not, then of the county or district from which the same shall have been taken; and they shall reside in their respective counties or districts during their terms of office.

Section 48. Time and place of meetings of legislature; maximum length of sessions.

The Legislature shall meet quadrennially at the Capitol in the Senate chamber, and in the Hall of the House of Representatives, on the second Tuesday in January next succeeding their election, or on such other day as may be prescribed by law; and shall not remain in session longer than sixty days at the first session held under the Constitution, nor longer than fifty days at any subsequent session. If at any time it should from any cause become impossible or dangerous for the Legislature to meet or remain at the Capitol or for the Senate to meet or remain in the

Senate Chamber, or for the Representatives to meet or remain in the Hall of the House of Representatives, the Governor may convene the Legislature, or remove it after it has convened, to some other place, or may designate some other place for the sitting of the respective Houses, or either of them, as necessity may require.

Section 49. Compensation of members of legislature.

The pay of the members of the Legislature shall be four dollars per day, and ten cents per mile in going to and returning from the seat of government, to be computed by the nearest usual route traveled.

Section 50. Number of senators and representatives; apportionment of legislators.

The Legislature shall consist of not more than thirty-five Senators, and not more than one hundred and five members of the House of Representatives, to be apportioned among the several districts and counties as prescribed in this Constitution; provided that in addition to the above number of Representatives, each new county hereafter created shall be entitled to one Representative.

Section 51. Election of president pro tem. of senate and speaker of house of representatives; temporary president and speaker; officers of each house; each house judge of election, returns and qualifications of members.

The Senate, at the beginning of each regular session, and at such other times as may be necessary, shall elect one of its members president pro tem thereof to preside over its deliberations in the absence of the Lieutenant-Governor; and the House of Representatives, at the beginning of each regular session, and at such other times as may be necessary, shall elect one of its members as Speaker; and the President of the Senate and the Speaker of the House of Representatives shall hold their offices respectively, until their successors are elected and qualified. In case of the temporary disability of either of said presiding officers, the House to which he belongs may elect one of its members to preside over that House and to perform all the duties of such officer during the continuance of his disability; and such temporary officer, while performing duty as such, shall receive the same compensation to which the permanent officer is entitled by law, and no other. Each House shall choose its own officers and shall judge of the election, returns and qualifications of its members.

Section 52. Quorum in each house.

A majority of each House shall constitute a quorum to do business; but a smaller number may adjourn from day to day and compel the attendance of absent members, in such manner and under such penalties as each House may provide.

Section 53. Rules of proceedings of both houses; punishment for contempt or disorderly behavior; enforcement of process; protection of members from violence, bribes, etc.; expulsion of members.

Each House shall have power to determine the rules of its proceedings and to punish its members and other persons, for contempt or disorderly behavior in its presence; to enforce obedience to its processes; to protect its members against violence, or offers of bribes or corrupct solicitation; and with the cncurrence of two-thirds of the House, to expel a member, but not a second time for the same offense; and the two Houses shall have all the powers necessary for the Legislature of a free State.

Section 54. Expulsion for corruption bar to further service in legislature; punishment for contempt or disorderly behavior not bar to indictment for same offense.

A member of the Legislature, expelled for corruption shall not thereafter be eligible to either House, and punishment for contempt or disorderly behavior shall not bar an indictment for the same offense.

Section 55. Journal of proceedings of each house.

Each House shall keep a Journal of its proceedings and cause the same to be published immediately after its adjournment, excepting such parts as, in its judgment, may require secrecy; and the yeas and nays of the members of either House on any question shall, at the request of one-tenth of the members present, be entered on the Journal. Any member of either House shall have liberty to dissent from or protest against any act or resolution which he may think injurious to the public, or to an individual, and have the reason for his dissent entered on the Journal.

Section 56. Immunity of legislators.

Members of the Legislature shall, in all cases, except treason, felony, violation of their oath of office, and breach of the peace, be privileged from arrest during their attendance at the session of their respective Houses, and in going to and returning from the same; and for any speech or debate in either House shall not be questioned in any other place.

Section 57. Doors of each house to be open; exceptions; restrictions on admittance to floor.

The doors of each House shall be opened except on such occasions as, in the opinion of the House, may require secrecy, but no person shall be admitted to the floor of either House while the same is in session, except members of the Legislature, the officers and employees of the two Houses, the Governor and his secretary, representatives of the press, and other persons to whom either House, by unanimous vote, may extend the privileges of its floor.

Section 58. Adjournment or change of place of sitting by one house without consent of other house.

Neither House shall, without consent of the other, adjourn for more than three days, nor to any other place than that in which they may be sitting except as otherwise provided in this Constitution.

Section 59. Appointment of legislators to other offices during terms for which elected.

No Senator or Representative shall, during the term for which he shall have been elected, be appointed to any office of profit under this State, which shall have been created, or the emoluments of which shall have been increased during such term, except such offices as may be filled by election by the people.

Section 60. Conviction of certain crimes bar to eligibility for legislature and to holding state office of trust or profit.

No person convicted of embezzlement of the public money, bribery, perjury, or other infamous crime, shall be eligible to the Legislature, or capable of holding any office of trust or profit in this State.

Section 61. Laws to be passed by bills; restrictions on amendments to bills.

No law shall be passed except by bill, and no bill shall be so altered or amended on its passage through either House as to change its original purpose.

Section 62. Referral of bills to standing committees.

No bill shall become a law until it shall have been referred to a standing committee of each House, acted upon by such committee in session, and returned therefrom, which facts shall affirmatively appear upon the Journal of each House.

Section 63. Number of readings for bills; recordation of votes on bills; majority vote required for passage of bills.

Every bill shall be read on three different days in each House, and no bill shall become a law, unless on its final passage it be read at length, and the vote be taken by yeas and nays, the names of the members voting for and against the same be entered upon the Journals, and a majority of each House be recorded thereon as voting in its favor, except as otherwise provided in this Constitution.

Section 64. Procedure for amendment of bills; adoption of reports of committees of conference.

No amendment to bills shall be adopted except by a majority of the House wherein the same is offered, nor unless the amendment with the names of those voting for and against the same shall be entered at length on the Journal of the House in which the same is adopted, and no amendment to bills by one House shall be concurred in by the other, unless a vote be taken by yeas and nays, and the names of the members voting for and against the same be recorded at length on the Journal; and no report of a committee of conference shall be adopted in either House, except upon a vote taken by yeas and nays, and entered on the Journal, as herein provided for the adoption of amendments.

Section 65. Lotteries and gift enterprises prohibited.

The Legislature shall have no power to authorize lotteries or gift enterprises for any purposes, and shall pass laws to prohibit the sale in this State of lottery or gift enterprise tickets, or tickets in any scheme in the nature of a lottery; and all acts, or parts of acts heretofore passed by the Legislature of this state, authorizing a lottery or lotteries, and all acts amendatory thereof, or supplemental thereto, are hereby avoided.

Section 66. Signature of bills by presiding officer of each house; reading of bills at length may be dispensed with.

The presiding officer of each House shall, in the presence of the House over which he presides, sign all bills and joint resolutions passed by the Legislature, after the same shall have been publicly read at length immediately before signing, and the fact of reading and signing shall be entered upon the Journal; but the reading at length may be dispensed with by a two-thirds vote of a quorum present, which fact shall also be entered on the Journal.

Section 67. Number, duties and compensation of officers and employees of each house.

The Legislature shall prescribe by law the number, duties, and compensation of the officers and employees of each House, and no payment shall be made from the State Treasury or be in any way authorized to any person except to an acting officer or employee elected or appointed in pursuance of law.

Section 68. Extra compensation not to be granted public officer, employee, contractor, etc., after service rendered or contract made; increase or decrease of compensation of officers during term of office.

The Legislature shall have no power to grant or to authorize or require any county or municipal authority to grant, nor shall any county or municipal authority have power to grant any extra compensation, fee, or allowance to any public officer, servant, or employee, agent or contractor, after service shall have been rendered or contract made, nor to increase or decrease the fees and compensation of such officers during their terms of office; nor shall any officer of the State bind the State to the payment of any sum of money but by authority of law; provided this section shall not apply to allowances made by commissioners' courts or boards of revenue to county officers for ex-officio services, nor prevent the Legislature from increasing or diminishing at any time the allowance to sheriffs or other officers for feeding, transferring, or guarding prisoners.

Section 69. Stationery, printing, fuel, etc., to be furnished by lowest responsible bidder; conflicts of interest.

All stationery, printing, paper, and fuel used in the legislative and other departments of government shall be furnished and the printing, binding, and distribution of laws, Journals, department reports, and all other printing, binding, and repairing and furnishing the halls and rooms used for the meeting of the Legislature and its committees, shall be performed under contract, to be given to the lowest responsible bidder below a maximum price, and under such regulations as shall be prescribed by law; no member or officer of any department of the government shall be in any way interested in such contract, and all such contracts shall be subject to the approval of the Governor, Auditor, and Treasurer.

Section 70. Revenue bills to originate in House of Representatives; preparation of general revenue bill; amendments to revenue bills by Senate; time limit for passage of revenue bills.

All bills for raising revenue shall originate in the House of Representatives. The Governor, Auditor, and Attorney General shall, before each regular session of the Legislature, prepare a general revenue bill to be submitted to the Legislature, for its information, and the Secretary of State shall have printed for the use of the Legislature a sufficient number of copies of the bill so prepared, which the Governor shall transmit to the House of Representatives as soon as organized, to be used or dealt with as that House may elect. The Senate may propose amendments to revenue bills. No revenue bill shall be passed during the last five days of the session.

Section 71. Restrictions on general appropriation bill.

The general appropriation bill shall embrace nothing but appropriations for the ordinary expenses of the Executive, Legislative, and Judicial departments of the State, for interest on the public debt, and for the public schools. The salary of no officer or employe shall be increased in such bill, nor shall any appropriation be made therein for any officer or employe unless his employment and the amount of his salary have already been provided for by law. All other appropriations shall be made by separate bills, each embracing but one subject.

Section 72. Payment of money out of state treasury; publication of annual statement of receipts and expenditures.

No money shall be paid out of the Treasury except upon appropriations made by law, and on warrant drawn by the proper officer in pursuance thereof; and a regular statement and account of receipts and expenditures of all public moneys shall be published annually, in such manner as may be by law directed.

Section 73. Appropriations to charitable or educational institutions not under absolute control of state.

No appropriation shall be made to any charitable or educational institution not under the absolute control of the State, other than normal schools established by law for the professional training of teachers for the public schools of the State, except by a vote of two-thirds of all the members elected to each House.

Section 74. Authorization of investment of trust funds by executors, trustees, etc., in bonds or stock of private corporations prohibited.

No act of the Legislature shall authorize the investment of any trust fund by executors, administrators, guardians, or other trustees in the bonds or stock of any private corporation; and any such acts now existing are avoided, saving investments heretofore made.

Section 75. Change of venue in civil and criminal cases.

The power to change the venue in civil and criminal causes is vested in the courts, to be exercised in such manner as shall be provided by law.

Section 76. Restrictions on legislation at special sessions; duration of special sessions.

When the Legislature shall be convened in special session, there shall be no legislation upon subjects other than those designated in the proclamation of the Governor calling such session, except by a vote of two-thirds of each house. Special sessions shall be limited to thirty days.

Section 77. State office for inspection or measuring of merchandise, commodities, etc., prohibited.

No State office shall be continued or created for the inspection or measuring of any merchandise, manufacture, or commodity, but any county or municipality may appoint such officers when authorized by law.

Section 78. Legislation to change seat of government of state.

No act of the Legislature changing the seat of government of the State shall become a law until the same shall have been submitted to the qualified electors of the State at a general election, and approved by a majority of such electors voting on the same; and such act shall specify the proposed new location.

Section 79. Bribery — Solicitation, acceptance, etc., of bribes by legislators.

A member of the Legislature who shall solicit, demand, or receive, or consent to receive, directly or indirectly, for himself or for another, from any company, corporation, association, or person, any money, office, appointment, employment, reward, thing of value, or enjoyment, or of personal advantage or promise thereof, for his vote or official influence, or for withholding the same; or with an understanding, expressed or implied, that his vote or official action shall be in any way influenced thereby; or who shall solicit or demand any such money or other advantage, matter, or thing aforesaid, for another as the consideration for his vote, or influence, or for withholding the same; or shall give or withhold his vote or influence in consideration of the payment or promise of such money, advantage, matter, or thing to another, shall be guilty of bribery within the meaning of this Constitution; and shall incur the disabilities and penalties provided thereby for such offense, and such additional punishment as is or shall be provided by law.

Section 80. Same — Offer, gift, etc., of money, etc., to executive or judicial officers or members of legislature to influence official acts.

Any person who shall, directly or indirectly, offer, give, or promise any money, or thing of value, testimonial, privilege, or personal advantage, to any executive or judicial officer or member of the Legislature to influence him in the performance of any of his public or official duties, shall be guilty of bribery, and be punished in such manner as may be provided by law.

Section 81. Offense of corrupt solicitation to be defined by law.

The offense of corrupt solicitation of members of the Legislature or of public officers of this state or of any municipal division thereof, and any occupation or practice of solicitation of such members or officers, to influence their official action, shall be defined by law, and shall be punished by fine and imprisonment in the penitentiary; and the Legislature shall provide for the trial and punishment of the offenses enumerated in the two preceding sections, and shall require the judges to give the same specially in charge to the grand juries in all the counties of this State.

Section 82. Disclosure of personal or private interest in bills, etc., by legislators.

A member of the Legislature who has a personal or private interest in any measure or bill proposed or pending before the Legislature, shall disclose the fact to the House of which he is a member, and shall not vote thereon.

Section 83. Voting in elections by legislature.

In all elections by the Legislature the members shall vote viva voce, and the votes shall be entered on the Journal.

Section 84. Adoption of laws to provide for arbitration between parties.

It shall be the duty of the Legislature to pass such laws as may be necessary and proper to decide differences by arbitrators to be appointed by the parties who may choose that mode of adjustment.

Section 85. Periodic revision and promulgation of laws.

It shall be the duty of the Legislature, at its first session after the ratification of this Constitution, and within every subsequent period of twelve years, to make provision by law for revising, digesting, and promulgating the public statutes of this State, of a general nature, both civil and criminal.

Section 86. Suppression of dueling.

The Legislature shall pass such penal laws as it may deem expedient to suppress the evil practice of dueling.

Section 87. Deductions from salaries or compensation of public officers for neglect of duty.

It shall be the duty of the Legislature to regulate by law the cases in which deduction shall be made from the salaries or compensation of public officers for neglect of duty in their official capacities, and the amount of such deduction.

Section 88. Counties to provide for maintenance of the poor.

It shall be the duty of the Legislature to require the several counties of this state to make adequate provision for the maintenance of the poor.

Section 89. Municipalities not to pass laws in conflict with general laws of state.

The Legislature shall not have power to authorize any municipal corporation to pass any laws inconsistent with the general laws of this State.

Section 90. Acquisition of foreign territory; rights and privileges of inhabitants of acquired territory.

In the event of the annexation of any foreign territory to this State, the Legislature shall enact laws extending to the inhabitants of the acquired territory all the rights and privileges which may be required by the terms of acquisition not inconsistent with this Constitution. Should the State purchase such foreign territory, the Legislature, with the approval of the Governor, shall be authorized to expend any money in the Treasury not otherwise appropriated, and, if necessary, to provide also for the issuance of State bonds, to pay for the purchase of such foreign territory.

Section 91. Exemption from taxation of state, county, municipal, cemetery and certain religious, educational and charitable property.

The legislature shall not tax the property, real or personal, of the State, counties, or other municipal corporations, or cemeteries; nor lots in incorporated cities and towns, or within one mile of any city or town to the extent of one acre, nor lots one mile or more distant from such cities or towns to the extent of five acres, with the buildings thereon, when same are used exclusively for religious worship, for schools, or for purposes purely charitable.

Section 92. Rules and regulations to ascertain value of property exempted from sale under legal process.

The Legislature shall by law prescribe such rules and regulations as may be necessary to ascertain the value of real and personal property exempted from sale under legal process by this Constitution, and to secure the same to the claimant thereof as selected.

Section 93. State not to engage in internal improvements or lend money or credit for same; state interest in private or corporate enterprises prohibited.

The State shall not engage in works of internal improvement, nor lend money or its credit in aid of such; nor shall the State be interested in any private or corporate enterprise, or lend money or its credit to any individual, association, or corporation.

Section 94. Municipalities not to grant public money or lend credit to private persons or corporations.

The Legislature shall not have power to authorize any county, city, town, or other subdivision of this State to lend its credit, or to grant public money or thing of value in aid of, or to any individual, association, or corporation whatsoever, or to become a stockholder in any such corporation, association, or company, by issuing bonds or otherwise.

Section 95. Impairing obligation of contracts; revival of barred rights or remedies; removal of cause of action or defense to suit after commencement of suit.

There can be no law of this State impairing the obligation of contracts by destroying or impairing the remedy for their enforcement; and the Legislature shall have no power to revive any right or remedy which may have become barred by lapse of time, or by any statute of this State. After suit has been commenced on any cause of action, the Legislature shall have no power to take away such cause of action, or destroy any existing defense to such suit.

Section 96. Uniformity of laws regulating court costs and charges and fees, commissions and allowances of public officers.

The Legislature shall not enact any law not applicable to all the counties in the State, regulating costs and charges of courts, or fees, commissions or allowances of public officers.

Section 97. Payment of salary of deceased officer after date of death.

The Legislature shall not authorize payment to any person of the salary of a deceased officer beyond the date of his death.

Section 98. Payments or grants to retiring officers.

The Legislature shall not retire any officer on pay, or part pay, or make any grant to such retiring officer.

Section 99. Restrictions on donation or sale of state lands to private corporations or individuals; grant of easements to railroad, telephone and telegraph companies.

Lands belonging to or under the control of the State shall never be donated, directly or indirectly, to private corporations, associations, or individuals, or railroad companies; nor shall such lands be sold to corporations or associations for a less price than that for which they are subject to sale to individuals; provided, that nothing contained in this section shall prevent the Legislature from granting a right of way, not exceeding one hundred and twenty-five feet in width, as a mere easement, for railroads or telegraph or telephone lines across State land, and the Legislature shall never dispose of the land covered by such right of way except subject to such easement.

Section 100. Obligations and liabilities of corporations, etc., held or owned by state, counties or municipalities.

No obligation or liability of any person, association, or corporation held or owned by this State, or by any county or other municipality thereof, shall ever be remitted, released, or postponed, or in any way diminished, by the Legislature; nor shall such liability or obligation be extinguished except by payment thereof; nor shall such liability or obligation be exchanged or transferred except upon payment of its face value; provided, that this section shall not prevent the Legislature from providing by general law for the compromise of doubtful claims.

Section 101. Lobbying in legislature by state or county officials.

No State or county official shall, at any time during his term of office, accept, either directly or indirectly, any fee, money, office, appointment, employment, reward, or thing of value, or of personal advantage, or the promise thereof, to lobby for or against any measure pending before the Legislature, or to give or withhold his influence to secure the passage or defeat of any such measure.

Section 102. Miscegenation laws.

The Legislature shall never pass any law to authorize or legalize any marriage between any white person and a negro, or descendant of a negro.

Section 103. Regulation, etc., of common carriers, partnerships, associations, trusts, monopolies and combinations of capital.

The Legislature shall provide by law for the regulation, prohibition, or reasonable restraint of common carriers, partnerships, associations, trusts, monopolies, and combinations of capital, so as to prevent them or any of them from making scarce articles of necessity, trade, or commerce, or from increasing unreasonably the cost thereof to the consumer, or preventing reasonable competition in any calling, trade, or business.

Section 104. Special, private or local laws — Prohibited in certain cases.

The Legislature shall not pass a special, private, or local law in any of the following cases:

1. Granting a divorce;

2. Relieving any minor of the disabilities of nonage;

3. Changing the name of any corporation, association, or individual;

4. Providing for the adoption or legitimizing of any child;

5. Incorporating a city, town, or village;

6. Granting a charter to any corporation, association, or individual;

7. Establishing rules of descent or distribution;
8. Regulating the time within which a civil or criminal action may be begun;

9. Exempting any individual, private corporation, or association from the operation of any general law;

10. Providing for the sale of the property of any individual or estate;

11. Changing or locating a county seat;

12. Providing for a change of venue in any case;

13. Regulating the rate of interest;

14. Fixing the punishment of crime;

15. Regulating either the assessment or collection of taxes, except in connection with the readjustment, renewal, or extension of existing municipal indebtedness created prior to the ratification of the Constitution of eighteen hundred and seventy-five;

16. Giving effect to an invalid will, deed, or other instrument;

17. Authorizing any county, city, town, village, district, or other political subdivision of a county, to issue bonds or other securities unless the issuance of said bonds or other securities shall have been authorized before the enactment of such local or special law, by a vote of the duly qualified electors of such county, township, city, town, village, district, or other political subdivision of a county, at an election held for such purpose, in the manner that may be prescribed by law; provided, the Legislature may, without such election, pass special laws to refund bonds issued before the date of the ratification of this Constitution;

18. Amending, confirming, or extending the charter of any private or municipal corporation, or remitting the forfeiture thereof; provided, this shall not prohibit the Legislature from altering or rearranging the boundaries of the city, town, or village;

19. Creating, extending, or impairing any lien;

20. Chartering or licensing any ferry, road, or bridge;

21. Increasing the jurisdiction and fees of justices of the peace or the fees of constables;

22. Establishing separate school districts;

23. Establishing separate stock districts;

24. Creating, increasing, or decreasing fees, percentages, or allowances of public officers;

25. Exempting property from taxation or from levy or sale;

26. Exempting any person from jury, road, or other civil duty;

27. Donating any lands owned by or under control of the State to any person or corporation;

28. Remitting fines, penalties, or forfeitures;

29. Providing for the conduct of elections or designating places of voting, or changing the boundaries of wards, precincts, or districts, except in the event of the organization of new counties, or the changing of the lines of old counties;

30. Restoring the right to vote to persons convicted of infamous crimes, or crimes involving moral turpitude;

31. Declaring who shall be liners between precincts or between counties.

The Legislature shall pass general laws for the cases enumerated in this section, provided that nothing in this section or article shall affect the right of the Legislature to enact local laws regulating or prohibiting the liquor traffic; but no such local law shall be enacted unless notice shall have been given as required in section 106 of this Constitution.

Section 105. Same Prohibited in cases provided for by general law; exception as to time of holding courts; partial repeal of general laws.

No special, private, or local law, except a law fixing the time of holding courts, shall be enacted in any case which is provided for by a general law, or when the relief sought can be given by any court of this State; and the courts, and not the Legislature, shall judge as to whether the matter of said law is provided for by a general law, and as to whether the relief sought can be given by any court; nor shall the Legislature indirectly enact any such special, private, or local law by the partial repeal of a general law.

Section 106. Same Publication or posting of notice of intent to apply therefor within county or counties affected prior to introduction of bill.

No special, private, or local law shall be passed on any subject not enumerated in section 104 of this Constitution, except in reference to fixing the time of holding courts, unless notice of the intention to apply therefor shall have been published, without cost to the State, in the county or counties where the matter or thing to be affected may be situated, which notice shall state the substance of the proposed law and be published at least once a week for four consecutive weeks in some newspaper published in such county or counties, or if there is no newspaper published therein, then by posting the said notice for four consecutive weeks at five different places in the county or counties prior to the introduction of the bill; and proof by affidavit that said notice has been given shall be exhibited to each house of the Legislature, and said proof spread upon the Journal. The courts shall pronounce void every special, private or local law which the Journals do not affirmatively show was passed in accordance with the provisions of this section.

Section 107. Same Notice required by section 106 prerequisite to repeal or amendment.

The Legislature shall not, by a special, private or local law, repeal or modify any special, private or local law except upon notice being given and shown as provided in the last preceding section.

Section 108. Suspension of general laws for benefit of individuals or private corporations; exemption of individuals or private corporations from operation of general laws.

The operation of a general law shall not be suspended for the benefit of any individual, private corporation or association; nor shall any individual, private corporation or association be exempted from the operation of any general law except as in this article otherwise provided.

Section 109. General laws for protection of local and private interests.

The Legislature shall pass general laws under which local and private interests shall be provided for and protected.

Section 110. "General law," "local law" and "special or private law" defined.

A general law within the meaning of this article is a law which applies to the whole State; a local law is a law which applies to any political subdivision or subdivisions of the State less than the whole; a special or private law within the meaning of this article is one which applies to an individual, association or corporation.

Section 111. Amendment of bill introduced as general law so as to become special, private or local law on passage.

No bill introduced as a general law in either House of the Legislature shall be so amended on its passage as to become a special, private or local law.

Article V: Executive Department

Section 112. Composition; officers enumerated.

The Executive department shall consist of a Governor, Lieutenant-Governor, Attorney General, State Auditor, Secretary of State, State Treasurer, Superintendent of Education, Commissioner of Agriculture and Industries, and a Sheriff for each county.

Section 113. Supreme executive power vested in Governor.

The supreme executive power of this State shall be vested in a chief magistrate, who shall be styled "The Governor of the State of Alabama."

Section 114. Governor, lieutenant governor, attorney-general, state auditor, secretary of state, state treasurer, superintendent of education and commissioner of agriculture and industries—How elected; when election held.

The Governor, Lieutenant-Governor, Attorney General, State Auditor, Secretary of State, State Treasurer, Superintendent of Education, and Commissioner of Agriculture and Industries shall be elected by the qualified electors of the State at the same time and places appointed for the election of members of the Legislature in the year nineteen hundred and two, and in every fourth year thereafter.

Section 115. Same Returns of election transmitted to speaker of house of representatives; opening and publication of election returns; duties of speaker and legislature ministerial in opening and publication of votes; person having highest number

The returns of every election for Governor, Lieutenant-Governor, Attorney General, State Auditor, Secretary of State, State Treasurer, Superintendent of Education, and Commissioner of Agriculture and Industries shall be sealed up and transmitted by the returning officers to the seat of government, directed to the Speaker of the House of Representatives, who shall, during the first week of the session to which such returns shall be made, open and publish them in the presence of both Houses of the Legislature in joint convention; but the Speaker's duty and the duty of the joint convention shall be purely ministerial. The result of the election shall be ascertained and declared by the Speaker from the face of the returns without delay. The person having the highest number of votes for any one of said offices shall be declared duly elected; but if two or more persons shall have an equal and the highest number of votes for the same office, the Legislature by joint vote, without delay, shall choose one of said persons for said office. Contested elections for Governor, Lieutenant-Governor, Attorney General, State Auditor, Secretary of State, State Treasurer, Superintendent of Education, and Commissioner of Agriculture and Industries shall be determined by both Houses of the Legislature in such manner as may be prescribed by law.

Section 116. Same Term of office; officers not eligible to succeed selves; governor not eligible for other state office or senate of United States during term or within one year thereafter.

The Governor, Lieutenant-Governor, Attorney General, State Auditor, Secretary of State, State Treasurer, Superintendent of Education, and Commissioner of Agriculture and Industries, elected after the ratification of this Constitution, shall hold their respective offices for the term of four years from the first Monday after the second Tuesday in January next succeeding their election, and until their successors shall be elected and qualified. After the first election under this Constitution no one of said officers shall be eligible as his own successor; and the Governor shall not be eligible to election or appointment to any office under this State, or to the Senate of the United States, during his term, and within one year after the expiration thereof.

Section 117. Qualifications of governor and lieutenant governor; lieutenant governor ex officio president of senate.

The Governor and Lieutenant-Governor shall each be at least thirty years of age when elected, and shall have been citizens of the United States ten years and resident citizens of this State at least seven years next before the date of their election. The Lieutenant-Governor shall be ex-officio President of the Senate, but shall have no right to vote except in the event of a tie.

Section 118. Compensation and residency requirements for governor, lieutenant governor, attorney-general, state auditor, secretary of state, state treasurer, superintendent of education and commissioner of agriculture and industries.

The Governor, Lieutenant-Governor, Attorney General, State Auditor, Secretary of State, State Treasurer, Superintendent of Education, and Commissioner of Agriculture and Industries shall receive compensation to be fixed by law, which shall not be increased or diminished during the term for which they shall have been elected, and shall, except the Lieutenant-Governor, reside at the State Capital during the time they continue in office, except during epidemics. The compensation of the Lieutenant-Governor shall be the same as that received by the Speaker of the House, except while serving as Governor, during which time his compensation shall be the same as that allowed the Governor.

Section 119. Increase in salary of governor at session of legislature following ratification of Constitution.

If the Legislature, at the session next after the ratification of this Constitution, shall enact a law increasing the salary of the Governor, such increase shall become effective and apply to the first Governor elected after the ratification of this Constitution, if the Legislature shall so determine.

Section 120. Governor to faithfully execute laws.

The Governor shall take care that the laws be faithfully executed.

Section 121. Governor may require reports from officers of executive department and officers and managers of state institutions; false reports or failure to file reports constitutes impeachable offense.

The Governor may require information in writing, under oath, from the officers of the executive department, named in this article, or created by statute, on any subject relating to the duties of their respective offices; and he may at any time require information in writing, under oath, from all officers and managers of State institutions, upon any subject relating to the condition, management and expenses of their respective offices and institutions. Any such officer or manager who makes a willfully false report or fails without sufficient excuse to make the required report on demand, is guilty of an impeachable offense.

Section 122. Governor authorized to convene legislature on extraordinary occasions; proclamation of governor to state matters on which action necessary.

The Governor may, by proclamation, on extraordinary occasions, convene the Legislature at the seat of government, or at a different place if, since their last adjournment, that shall have become dangerous from an enemy, insurrection, or other lawless outbreak, or from any infectious or contagious disease; and he shall state specifically in such proclamation each matter concerning which the action of that body is deemed necessary.

Section 123. Reports and information to be given legislature by governor; presentation of budget to legislature.

The Governor shall, from time to time, give to the Legislature information of the state of the government, and recommend for its consideration such measures as he may deem expedient; and at the commencement of each regular session of the Legislature, and at the close of his term of office, he shall give information by written message of the condition of the State; and he shall account to the Legislature, as may be prescribed by law, for all moneys received and paid out by him or by his order; and at the commencement of each regular session he shall present to the Legislature estimates of the amount of money required to be raised by taxation for all purposes.

Section 124. Authority of governor to remit fines and forfeitures and grant reprieves, paroles, commutations of sentence and pardons; board of pardons; report by governor to legislature; pardons in cases of felonies and offenses involving moral turpitud.

The Governor shall have power to remit fines and forfeitures, under such rules and regulations as may be prescribed by law; and, after conviction, to grant reprieves, paroles, commutations of sentence and pardons, except in cases of impeachment. The Attorney General, Secretary of State, and State Auditor shall constitute a Board of Pardons, who shall meet on the call of the Governor, and before whom shall be laid all recommendations or petitions, for pardon, commutation or parole, in cases of felony; and the board shall hear them in open session, and give their opinion thereon in writing to the Governor, after which or on the failure of the board to advise for more than sixty days, the Governor may grant or refuse the commutation, parole or pardon, as to him seems best for the public interest. He shall communicate to the Legislature at each session every remission of fines and forfeitures, and every reprieve, commutation, parole, or pardon, with his reasons therefor, and the opinion of the Board of Pardons in each case required to be referred, stating the name and crime of the convict, the sentence, its date, and the date of reprieve, commutation, parole, or pardon. Pardons in cases of felony and other offenses involving moral turpitude shall not relieve from civil and political disabilities, unless approved by the Board of Pardons and specifically expressed in the pardon.

Section 125. Presentation of bills to governor for signature; veto power of governor; procedure for passage of bill after veto by governor; effect of failure of governor to sign bill.

Every bill which shall have passed both Houses of the Legislature, except as otherwise provided in this Constitution, shall be presented to the Governor; if he approve, he shall sign it; but if not, he shall return it with his objections to the House in which it originated, which shall enter the objections at large upon the Journal and proceed to reconsider it. If the Governor's message proposes no amendment which would remove his objections to the bill, the House in which the bill originated may proceed to reconsider it, and if a majority of the whole number elected to that House vote for the passage of the bill, it shall be sent to the other House, which shall in like manner reconsider, and if a majority of the whole number elected to that House vote for the passage of the bill, the same shall become a law, notwithstanding the Governor's veto. If the Governor's message proposes amendment, which would remove his objections, the House to which it is sent may so amend the bill and send it with the Governor's message to the other House, which may adopt, but cannot amend, said amendment; and both Houses concurring in the amendment, the bill shall again be sent to the Governor and acted on by him as other bills. If the House to which the bill is returned refuses to make such amendment, it shall proceed to reconsider it; and if a majority of the whole number elected to that House shall vote for the passage of the bill, it shall be sent with the objections to the other House, by which it shall likewise be reconsidered, and if approved by a majority of the whole number elected to that House, it shall become a law. If the House to which the bill is returned makes the amendment, and the other House declines to pass the same, that House shall proceed to reconsider it, as though the bill had originated therein, and such proceedings shall be taken thereon as above provided. In every such case the vote of both Houses shall be determined by yeas and nays, and the names of the members voting for or against the bill shall be entered upon the Journals of each House respectively. If any bill shall not be returned by the Governor within six days, Sunday excepted, after it shall have been presented, the same shall become a law in like manner as if he had signed it, unless the Legislature, by its adjournment, prevent the return, in which case it shall not be a law; but when return is prevented by recess, such bill must be returned to the House in which it originated within two days after the reassembling, otherwise it shall become a law, but bills presented to the Governor within five days before the final adjournment of the Legislature may be approved by the Governor at any time within ten days after such adjournment, and if approved and deposited with the Secretary of State within that time shall become law. Every vote, order, or resolution to which concurrence of both Houses may be necessary, except on questions of adjournment and the bringing on of elections by the two Houses, and amending this Constitution, shall be presented to the Governor; and, before the same shall take effect, be approved by him; or, being disapproved, shall be repassed by both Houses according to the rules and limitations prescribed in the case of a bill.

Section 126. Authority of governor to veto items in appropriation bills.

The Governor shall have power to approve or disapprove any item or items of any appropriation bill embracing distinct items, and the part or the parts of the bill approved shall be the law, and the item or items disapproved shall be void, unless repassed according to the rules and limitations prescribed for the passage of bills over the executive veto; and he shall in writing state specifically the item or items he disapproves, setting the same out in full in his message, but in such case the enrolled bill shall not be returned with the Governor's objection.

Section 127. Succession to office of governor; filling of vacancy when offices of governor and lieutenant governor both vacant; procedure when governor or successor impeached, absent from state, disabled, etc.; failure of governor-elect, lieutenant gove

In case of the Governor's removal from office, death or resignation, the Lieutenant-Governor shall become Governor. If both the Governor and Lieutenant-Governor be removed from office, die, or resign more than sixty days prior to the next general election at which any State officers are to be elected, a Governor and Lieutenant-Governor shall be elected at such election for the unexpired term, and in the event of a vacancy in the office, caused by the removal from office, death or resignation of the Governor and Lieutenant-Governor, pending such vacancy and until their successors shall be elected and qualified, the office of Governor shall be held and administered by either the President pro tem of the Senate, Speaker of the House of Representatives, Attorney General, State Auditor, Secretary of State, or State Treasurer in the order herein named. In case of the impeachment of the Governor, his absence from the State for more than twenty days, unsoundness of mind, or other disability, the power and authority of the office shall, until the Governor is acquitted, returns to the State, or is restored to his mind, or relieved from other disability, devolve in the order herein named, upon the Lieutenant-Governor, President pro tem of the Senate, Speaker of the House of Representatives, Attorney General, State Auditor, Secretary of State, and State Treasurer. If any of these officers be under any of the disabilities herein specified, the office of the Governor shall be administered in the order named by such of these officers as may be free from such disability. If the Governor shall be absent from the State over twenty days, the Secretary of State shall notify the Lieutenant-Governor, who shall enter upon the duties of Governor; if both the Governor and Lieutenant-Governor shall be absent from the State over twenty days, the Secretary of State shall notify the President pro tem of the Senate, who shall enter upon the duties of Governor, and so on, in case of such absence, shall notify each of the other officers named in their order, who shall discharge the duties of the office until the Governor or other officer entitled to administer the office in succession to the Governor returns. If the Governor-elect fails or refuse from any cause to qualify, the Lieutenant-Governor-elect shall qualify and exercise the duties of Governor until the Governor-elect qualifies; and in the event both the Governor-elect and the Lieutenant-Governor-elect from any cause fail to qualify, the President pro tem of the Senate, the Speaker of the House of Representatives, the Attorney General, State Auditor, Secretary of State, and State Treasurer shall in like manner, in the order named, administer the office, until the Governor-elect or Lieutenant-Governor-elect qualifies.

Section 128. Procedure when governor or acting governor appears to be of unsound mind.

If the Governor or other officer administering the office shall appear to be of unsound mind, it shall be the duty of the Supreme Court of Alabama, at any regular term, or at any special term, which it is hereby authorized to call for that purpose, upon request in writing, verified by their affidavits, of any two of the officers named in Section 127 of this Constitution, not next in succession to the office of Governor, to ascertain the mental condition of the Governor or other officer administering the office, and if he is adjudged to be of unsound mind, to so decree, a copy of which decree, duly certified, shall be filed in the office of Secretary of State; and in the event of such adjudication it shall be the duty of the officer next in succession to perform the duties of the office until the Governor or other officer administering the office is restored to his mind. If the incumbent denies that the Governor or other person entitled to administer the office has been restored to his mind, the Supreme

Court, at the instance of any officer named in Section 127 of this Constitution, shall ascertain the truth concerning the same, and if the officer has been restored to his mind, shall so adjudge and file a duly certified copy of its decree with the Secretary of State; and in the event of such adjudication, the office shall be restored to him. The Supreme Court shall prescribe the method of taking testimony and the rules of practice in such proceedings, which rules shall include a provision for the service of notice of such proceedings on the Governor or person acting as Governor.

Section 129. Compensation of acting governor.

The Lieutenant-Governor, President pro tem of the Senate, Speaker of the House, Attorney General, State Auditor, Secretary of State, or State Treasurer, while administering the office of Governor, shall receive like compensation as that prescribed by law for the Governor, and no other.

Section 130. Holding office in addition to that of governor.

No person shall at the same time hold the office of Governor and any other office, civil or military, under this State, or the United States, or any other State or government, except as otherwise provided in this Constitution.

Section 131. Military powers of governor.

The Governor shall be commander-in-chief of the militia and volunteer forces of this State, except when they shall be called into the service of the United States, and he may call out the same to execute the laws, suppress insurrection and repel invasion, but need not command in person unless directed to do so by resolution of the Legislature; and when acting in the service of the United States, he shall appoint his staff, and the Legislature shall fix his rank.

Section 132. Qualifications of attorney-general, state auditor, secretary of state, state treasurer, superintendent of education and commissioner of agriculture and industries.

No person shall be eligible to the office of Attorney General, State Auditor, Secretary of State, State Treasurer, Superintendent of Education, or Commissioner of Agriculture and Industries unless he shall have been a citizen of the United States at least seven years, and shall have resided in this State at least five years next preceding his election, and shall be at least twenty-five years old when elected.

Section 133. Great seal of state.

There shall be a seal of the State which shall be used officially by the Governor, and the seal now in use shall continue to be used until another shall have been adopted by the Legislature. The seal shall be called "The Great Seal of the State of Alabama."

Section 134. Duties of secretary of state generally.

The Secretary of State shall be the custodian of the Great Seal of the State, and shall authenticate therewith all official acts of the Governor, except his approval of laws, resolutions, appointments to office, and administrative orders. He shall keep a register of the official acts of the Governor, and when necessary, shall attest them, and lay copies of same together with copies of all papers relative thereto, before either House of the Legislature when required to do so, and shall perform such other duties as may be prescribed by law.

Section 135. Issuance and execution of grants and commissions.

All grants and commissions shall be issued in the name and by the authority of the State of Alabama, sealed with the Great Seal of the State, signed by the Governor and countersigned by the Secretary of State.

Section 136. Vacancy in office or unsoundness of mind of attorney-general, state auditor, secretary of state, state treasurer, superintendent of education or commissioner of agriculture and industries.

Should the office of Attorney General, State Auditor, Secretary of State, State Treasurer, Superintendent of Education, or Commissioner of Agriculture and Industries become vacant from any cause, the Governor shall fill such vacancy until the disability is removed or a successor elected and qualified. In case any of said officers shall become of unsound mind, such unsoundness shall be ascertained by the Supreme Court upon the suggestion of the Governor.

Section 137. Duties generally and restrictions on receipt of fees, etc., by attorney-general, state auditor, secretary of state, state treasurer, superintendent of education and commissioner of agriculture and industries; annual report by state treasure

The Attorney General, State Auditor, Secretary of State, State Treasurer, Superintendent of Education, and Commissioner of Agriculture and Industries shall perform such duties as may be prescribed by law. The State Treasurer and State Auditor shall every year, at a time fixed by the Legislature, make a full and complete report to the Governor, showing the receipts and disbursements of every character, all claims audited and paid out, by items, and all taxes and revenues collected and paid into the treasury, and the sources thereof. They shall make reports oftener upon any matters pertaining to their offices, if required by the Governor or the Legislature. The Attorney General, State Auditor, Secretary of State, State Treasurer, and Commissioner of Agriculture and Industries shall not receive to their use any fees, costs, perquisites of office or other compensation than the salaries prescribed by law, and all fees that may be payable for any services performed by such officers shall be at once paid into the State Treasury.

Section 138. Election and term of office of sheriffs; sheriff not eligible to succeed self; impeachment of sheriff; effect of impeachment of sheriff.

A Sheriff shall be elected in each county by the qualified electors thereof, who shall hold office for a term of four years, unless sooner removed, and he shall be ineligible to such office as his own successor; provided, that the terms of all Sheriffs expiring in the year nineteen hundred and four are hereby extended until the time of the expiration of the terms of the other executive officers of this State in the year nineteen hundred and seven, unless sooner removed. Whenever any prisoner is taken from jail, or from the custody of any Sheriff or his deputy, and put to death, or suffers grievous bodily harm, owing to the neglect, connivance, cowardice or other grave fault of the Sheriff, such Sheriff may be impeached under Section 174 of this Constitution. If the Sheriff be impeached, and thereupon convicted, he shall not be eligible to hold any office in this State during the time for which he had been elected or appointed to serve as sheriff.

Article VI: Judicial Department

Section 139. Vesting of judicial power; minimum standards for establishment of courts of general jurisdiction in counties.

The judicial power of the State shall be vested in the Senate sitting as a court of impeachment, a Supreme Court, Circuit Courts, Chancery Courts, Courts of Probate, such courts of law and equity inferior to the Supreme Court, and to consist of not more than five members, as the Legislature from time to time may establish, and such persons as may be by law invested with powers of a judicial nature; but no court of general jurisdiction, at law or in equity, or both, shall hereafter be established in and for any one county having a population of less than twenty thousand, according to the next preceding Federal census, and property assessed for taxation at a less valuation than three million five hundred thousand dollars.

Section 140. Jurisdiction of supreme court generally; power of supreme court to issue certain remedial and original writs.

Except in cases otherwise directed in this Constitution, the Supreme Court shall have appellate jurisdiction only, which shall be coextensive with the State, under such restrictions and regulations, not repugnant to this Constitution, as may from time to time be prescribed by law, except where jurisdiction over appeals is vested in some inferior court, and made final therein; provided, that the Supreme Court shall have power to issue writs of injunction, habeas corpus, quo warranto, and such other remedial and original writs as may be necessary to give it a general superintendence and control of inferior jurisdictions.

Section 141. Place of holding supreme court.

The Supreme Court shall be held at the seat of government, but if that shall become dangerous from any cause, it may convene at or adjourn to another place.

Section 142. Division of state into circuits; residency requirements for circuit judges.

Except as otherwise authorized in this article, the State shall be divided into convenient circuits. For each circuit there shall be chosen a judge, who shall for one year next preceding his election and during his continuance in office, reside in the circuit for which he is elected.

Section 143. Jurisdiction of circuit courts.

The Circuit Court shall have original jurisdiction in all matters civil and criminal within the State not otherwise excepted in this Constitution; but in civil cases, other than suits for libel, slander, assault and battery, and ejectment, it shall have no original jurisdiction except where the matter or sum in controversy exceeds fifty dollars.

Section 144. When and where circuit courts to be held; circuit judges may hold court for each other; power of circuit judges to issue writs of injunction returnable to courts of chancery.

A Circuit Court, or a court having the jurisdiction of the Circuit Court, shall be held in each county in the state at least twice in every year, and judges of the several courts mentioned in this section may hold court for each other when they deem it expedient, and shall do so when directed by law. The judges of the several courts mentioned in this section shall have power to issue writs of injunction, returnable to the Courts of Chancery, or courts having the jurisdiction of Courts of Chancery.

Section 145. Authority to establish courts of chancery; division of state into chancery divisions; districts within chancery divisions; residency requirements for chancellor.

The Legislature shall have power to establish a Court or Courts of Chancery, with original and appellate jurisdiction, except as otherwise authorized in this article. The state shall be divided by the legislature into convenient Chancery divisions; each division shall be divided into districts, and for each division there shall be a chancellor, who shall have resided in the division for which he shall be elected or appointed, for one year next preceding his election or appointment, and shall reside therein during his continuance in office.

Section 146. When and where chancery courts to be held; chancellors may hold court for each other.

A Chancery Court, or a court having the jurisdiction of the Chancery Court, shall be held in each district, at a place to be fixed by law, at least twice in each year, and the chancellors may hold court for each other when they deem it necessary, and shall do so when directed by law.

Section 147. Certain counties need not be included in circuit or chancery divisions; minimum number of counties in circuit or chancery divisions.

Any county having a population of twenty thousand or more, according to the next preceding Federal census, and also taxable property of three million five hundred thousand dollars or more in value, according to the next preceding assessment of property for State and county taxation, need not be included in any circuit or chancery division; but if the value of its taxable property shall be reduced below that limit, or if its population shall be reduced below that number, the Legislature shall include such county in a circuit and chancery division, or either, embracing more than one county. No Circuit or Chancery division shall contain less than three counties, unless there be embraced therein a county having a population of twenty thousand or more, and taxable property of three million five hundred thousand dollars or more in value.

Section 148. Legislature may confer jurisdiction of circuit and chancery court on either court; consolidation of courts in counties having two or more courts of record.

The Legislature may confer upon the Circuit Court or the Chancery Court the jurisdiction of both of said courts. In counties having two or more courts of record, the Legislature may provide for the consolidation of all or any such courts of record, except the Probate Court, with or without separate divisions, and a sufficient number of judges for the transaction of the business of such consolidated court.

Section 149. Legislature may establish court of probate in each county; powers generally of probate courts.

The Legislature shall have power to establish in each county a court of probate, with general jurisdiction of orphan's business and with power to grant letters testamentary and administration; provided, that whenever any court having equity powers has taken jurisdiction of the settlement of any estate, it shall have power to do all things necessary for the settlement of such estate, including the appointment and removal of administrators, executors, guardians and trustees, and including action upon the resignation of either of them.

Section 150. Compensation and restrictions on holding other offices for supreme court justices, chancellors and judges of circuit and other courts of record, except probate judges.

The Justices of the Supreme Court, Chancellors, and the Judges of the Circuit Courts and other courts of record, except Probate Courts, shall, at stated times, receive for their services a compensation which shall not be diminished during their official terms; they shall receive no fees or perquisites, nor hold any office, except judicial offices, of profit or trust under this State or the United States, or any other government, during the time for which they have been elected or appointed.

Section 151. Composition of supreme court.

The Supreme Court shall consist of one Chief Justice and such number of Associate Justices as may be prescribed by law.

Section 152. Election of supreme court justices, judges of circuit courts, judges of probate courts and chancellors.

The Chief Justice and Associate Justices of the Supreme Court, Judges of the Circuit Courts, Judges of Probate Courts, and Chancellors shall be elected by the qualified electors of the State, circuits, counties and chancery divisions, for which such courts may be established, at such times as may be prescribed by law, except as herein otherwise provided.

Section 153. Election or appointment of judges of inferior courts.

The Judges of such inferior courts of law and equity as may be by law established, shall be elected or appointed in such mode as the Legislature may prescribe.

Section 154. Qualifications of chancellors and judges of courts of record.

Chancellors and Judges of all courts of record shall have been citizens of the United States and of this State for five years next preceding their election or appointment, and shall be not less than twenty-five years of age, and, except Judges of Probate Courts, shall be learned in the law.

Section 155. Terms of office of supreme court justices, chancellors and judges of circuit and probate courts.

Except as otherwise provided in this article, the Chief Justice and Associate Justices of the Supreme Court, Circuit Judges, Chancellors, and Judges of Probate, shall hold office for the term of six years, and until their successors are elected or appointed, and qualified; and the right of such Judges and Chancellors to hold their offices for the full term hereby prescribed shall not be affected by any change hereafter made by law in any circuit, division or county, or in the mode or time of election.

Section 156. Time of holding election for supreme court justices; staggered terms of office for supreme court justices.

The Chief Justice and Associate Justices of the Supreme Court shall be choses at an election to be held at the time and places fixed by law for the election of members of the House of Representatives of the Congress of the United States, until the Legislature shall by law change the time of holding such election. The term of office of the Chief Justice, who shall be elected in the year nineteen hundred and four, shall be as provided in the last preceding section. The successors of two of the Associate Justices elected in the year nineteen hundred and four shall be elected in the year nineteen hundred and six, and the successors of the other two Associate Justices elected in nineteen hundred and four, shall be elected in the year nineteen hundred and eight. The Associate Justices of said court elected in the year nineteen hundred and four shall draw or cast lots among themselves to determine which of them shall hold office for the terms ending, respectively, in the years nineteen hundred and six and nineteen hundred and eight, and until their respective successors are elected or appointed and qualified. The result of such determination shall be certified to the Governor by such Associate Justices, or a majority of them, prior to the first day of January, nineteen hundred and five, and such certificate shall be entered upon the minutes of the court. In the event of the failure of said Associate Justices to make and certify such determination, the Governor shall designate the terms for which they shall respectively hold office, as above provided, and shall issue his proclamation accordingly. In the event of an increase or reduction by law of the number of Associate Justices of the Supreme Court, the Legislature shall, as nearly as may be, provide for the election, each second year, of one-third of the members of said court.

Section 157. Judicial officers conservators of the peace.

All judicial officers within their respective jurisdictions shall, by virtue of their offices, be conservators of the peace.

Section 158. Vacancies in office of supreme court justices, elected judges and chancellors.

Vacancies in the office of any of the Justices of the Supreme Court or Judges who hold office by election, or Chancellors of this State, shall be filled by appointment by the Governor. The appointee shall hold his office until the next general election for any State officer held at least six months after the vacancy occurs, and until his successor is elected and qualified; the successor chosen at such election shall hold office for the unexpired term and until his successor is elected and qualified.

Section 159. Initial appointment or election of judges or chancellors for newly created circuits or chancery divisions.

Whenever any new circuit or chancery division is created the Judge or Chancellor therefor shall be elected at the next general election for any State officer for a term to expire at the next general election for Circuit Judge and Chancellors; provided, that if said new circuit or chancery division is created more than six months before such general election for any State officer, the Governor shall appoint some one as Judge or Chancellor, as the case may be, to hold the office until such election.

Section 160. Procedure when judge or chancellor incompetent to try, hear or render judgment in case.

If in any case, civil or criminal, pending in any Circuit Court, Chancery Court, or in any court of general jurisdiction having any part of the jurisdiction of a Circuit and a Chancery Court, or either of them in this State, the presiding judge or chancellor shall, for any legal cause, be incompetent to try, hear or render judgment in such case, the parties, or their attorneys of record, if it be a civil case, or the solicitor or prosecuting officer, and the defendant or defendants, if it be a criminal case, may agree upon some disinterested person practicing in the court and learned in the law, to act as a special judge or chancellor to sit as a court, and to hear, decide, and render judgment in the same manner and to the same effect as such incompetent Chancellor or Judge could have rendered but for such incompetency. If the case be a civil one, and the parties or their attorneys of record do not agree; or if it be a criminal one, and the prosecuting officer and the defendant or defendants do not agree upon a special judge or chancellor, or if either party in a civil cause is not represented in court, the Register in Chancery or the clerk of such Circuit or other court in which said cause is pending, shall appoint a special judge or chancellor, who shall preside, try and render judgment as in this section provided. The Legislature may prescribe other methods for supplying special judges in such cases.

Section 161. Failure of judges or chancellors to attend regular terms of court.

The Legislature shall have power to provide for the holding of Chancery and Circuit Courts, and for the holding of courts having the jurisdiction of Circuit and Chancery Courts, or either of them, when the Chancellors or Judges thereof fail to attend regular terms.

Section 162. Judges of courts of record not to practice law.

No Judge of any court of record in this State shall practice law in any of the courts of this State or of the United States.

Section 163. Appointment, qualifications, terms of office and compensation of registers in chancery; fees of registers of chancery to be uniform throughout state.

Registers in Chancery shall be appointed by the Chancellors of the respective divisions, and shall have been at least twelve months before their appointment, and shall be at the time of their appointment and during their continuance in office, resident citizens of the district for which they are appointed. They shall hold office for the term for which the Chancellors making such appointment was elected or appointed. Such registers shall receive as compensation for their services only such fees and commissions as may be specifically prescribed by law, which fees shall be uniform throughout the State.

Section 164. Appointment and term of office of clerk of supreme court; selection of clerks of inferior courts.

The clerk of the Supreme Court shall be appointed by the Judges thereof, and shall hold office for the term of six years; and the clerks of such inferior courts as may be established by law shall be selected in such manner as the Legislature may provide.

Section 165. Election and term of office of clerks of circuit courts; clerk may serve as register in chancery; filling of vacancies in office of clerk.

Clerks of the Circuit Court shall be elected by the qualified electors in each county for the term of six years, and may, when appointed by the Chancellor, also fill the office of Register in Chancery. Vacancies in such office of clerk shall be filled by the Judge of the Circuit Court for the unexpired term.

Section 166. Removal of clerk of supreme court and registers in chancery.

The clerk of the Supreme Court and Registers in Chancery may be removed from office by the Justices of the Supreme Court, and by the Chancellors, respectively, for cause, to be entered at length upon the minutes of the court.

Section 167. Election, qualifications, terms of office and compensation of circuit solicitors; appointment or election of county solicitors.

A Solicitor for each judicial circuit or other territorial subdivision prescribed by the Legislature, shall be elected by the qualified electors of those counties in such circuit or other territorial subdivision in which such Solicitor prosecutes criminal cases, and such Solicitor shall be learned in the law, and shall at the time of his election and during his continuance in office, reside in a county (in the circuit) in which he prosecutes criminal cases, or other territorial subdivision for which he is elected, and his term of office shall be for four years, and he shall receive no other compensation than a salary, to be prescribed by law, which shall not be increased during the term for which he was elected; provided, that this article shall not operate to abridge the term of any Solicitor now in office; and, provided further, that the Solicitors elected in the year nineteen hundred and four shall hold office for six years, and until their successors are elected and qualified; and provided further, that the Legislature may provide by law for the appointment by the Governor or the election by the qualified electors of a county for a Solicitor for any county.

Section 168. Election of justices of the peace and constables; jurisdiction of justices of the peace; fees of justices of the peace and constables; appeals from justices of the peace; terms of office of justices of the peace and notaries public; appoint

In each precinct not lying within, or partly within, any city or incorporated town of more than fifteen hundred inhabitants, there shall be elected by the qualified electors of such precinct not exceeding two Justices of the Peace, and one Constable. Where one or more precincts lie within, or partly within, a city or incorporated town having more than fifteen hundred inhabitants, the Legislature may provide by law for the election of not more than two Justice of the Peace and one Constable, for each of such precincts, or an inferior court for such precinct or precincts, in lieu of all Justices of the Peace therein. Justices of the Peace, and the inferior courts in this section provided for, shall have jurisdiction in all civil cases where the amount in controversy does not exceed one hundred dollars, except in cases of libel, slander, assault and battery, and ejectment. The Legislature may provide by law what fees may be charged by Justices of the Peace and Constables, which fees shall be uniform throughout the State. The right of appeal from any judgment of a Justice of the Peace, or from any inferior court authorized by this section, without the prepayment of costs, and also the term of office of such Justices, and the Judges of such inferior courts, and of Notaries Public, shall be provided for by law. The Governor may appoint Notaries Public without the powers of a Justice of the Peace, and may, except where otherwise provided by an act of the Legislature, appoint not more than one Notary Public with all of the powers and jurisdiction of a Justice of the Peace for each precinct in which the election of Justices of the Peace shall be authorized.

Section 169. Exclusion of persons from courtroom in cases of rape and assault with intent to ravish.

In all prosecutions for rape and assault with intent to ravish, the court may, in its discretion, exclude from the court room all persons, except such as may be necessary in the conduct of the trial.

Section 170. Style of all processes.

The style of all processes shall be "The State of Alabama," and all prosecutions shall be carried on in the name and by the authority of the same, and shall conclude "Against the peace and dignity of the State."

Section 171. Authority of legislature to abolish courts when function conferred upon some other court.

The Legislature shall have the power to abolish any court, except the Supreme Court and the Probate Courts, whenever its jurisdiction and functions have been conferred upon some other court.

Section 172. Terms of office of incumbents not abridged.

Nothing in this article shall be so construed as to abridge the term of office of any officer now in office.

Article VII: Impeachments

Section 173. Governor, lieutenant-governor, attorney-general, state auditor, secretary of state, state treasurer, superintendent of education, commissioner of agriculture and industries and justices of supreme court.

The Governor, Lieutenant-Governor, Attorney General, State Auditor, Secretary of State, State Treasurer, Superintendent of Education, Commissioner of Agriculture and Industries, and Justices of the Supreme Court may be removed from office for willful neglect of duty, corruption in office, incompetency, or intemperance in the use of intoxicating liquors or narcotics to such an extent, in view of the dignity of the office and importance of its duties, as unfits the officer for the discharge of such duties, or for any offense involving moral turpitude while in office, or committed under color thereof, or connected therewith, by the Senate sitting as a court of impeachment, under oath or affirmation, on articles or charges preferred by the House of Representatives. When the Governor or Lieutenant-Governor is impeached, the Chief Justice, or if he be absent or disqualified, then one of the Associate Justices of the Supreme Court, to be selected by it, shall preside over the Senate when sitting as a court of impeachment. If at any time when the Legislature is not in session, a majority of all the members elected to the House of Representatives shall certify in writing to the Secretary of State their desire to meet to consider the impeachment of the Governor, Lieutenant-Governor, or other officer administering the office of Governor, it shall be the duty of the Secretary of State immediately to notify the Speaker of the House, who shall, within ten days after receipt of such notice, summon the members of the House, by publication in some newspaper published at the Capital, to assemble at the Capitol on a day to be fixed by the Speaker, not later than fifteen days after the receipt of the notice to him from the Secretary of State, to consider the impeachment of the Governor, Lieutenant-Governor, or other officer administering the office of Governor. If the House of Representatives prefer articles of impeachment, the Speaker of the House shall forthwith notify the Lieutenant-Governor, unless he be the officer impeached, in which event he shall notify the Secretary of State, who shall summon, in the manner herein above provided for, the members of the Senate to assemble at the Capitol on a day to be named in said summons, not later than ten days after receipt of the notice from the Speaker of the House, for the purpose of organizing as a court of impeachment. The Senate, when thus organized, shall hear and try such articles of impeachment against the Governor, Lieutenant-Governor or other officer administering the office of Governor, as may be preferred by the House of Representatives.

Section 174. Chancellors, judges of circuit and probate courts, judges of courts from which appeal may be taken directly to supreme court, solicitors and sheriffs.

The Chancellors, Judges of the Circuit Courts, Judges of the Probate Courts, and Judges of other courts from which an appeal may be taken directly to the Supreme Court, and Solicitors and Sheriffs, may be removed from office for any of the causes specified in the preceding section or elsewhere in this Constitution, by the Supreme Court, under such regulations as may be prescribed by law. The Legislature may provide for the impeachment or removal of other officers than those named in this article.

Section 175. Clerks of circuit courts, courts of like jurisdiction and criminal courts, tax collectors, tax assessors, judges of inferior courts, coroners, justices of the peace, notaries public, constables and county and municipal officers.

The clerks of the Circuit Courts, or courts of like jurisdiction, and of Criminal Courts, Tax Collectors, Tax Assessors, County Treasurers, County Superintendents of Education, Judges of inferior courts created under authority of Section 168 of this Constitution, Coroners, Justices of the Peace, Notaries Public, Constables, and all other county officers, Mayors, Intendants, and all other officers of incorporated cities and towns in this State, may be removed from office for any of the causes specified in Section 173 of this Constitution, by the Circuit or other courts of like jurisdiction or a Criminal Court of the county in which such officers hold their office, under such regulations as may be prescribed by law; provided, that the right of trial by jury and appeal in such cases shall be secured.

Section 176. Limitation on impeachment penalties; accused person liable to indictment and punishment.

The penalties in cases arising under the three preceding sections shall not extend beyond removal from office, and disqualifications from holding office, under the authority of this State, for the term for which the officer was elected or appointed; but the accused shall be liable to indictment and punishment as prescribed by law.

Article VIII: Suffrage and Elections

Section 177. Age and citizenship qualifications of electors.

Every male citizen of this State who is a citizen of the United States, and every male resident of foreign birth, who, before the ratification of this Constitution, shall have legally declared his intention to become a citizen of the United States, 21 years old or upwards, not laboring under any of the disabilities named in this article, and possessing the qualifications required by it, shall be an elector, and shall be entitled to vote at any election by the people; provided, that all foreigners who have legally declared their intention to become citizens of the United States, shall, if they fail to become citizens thereof at the time they are entitled to become such, cease to have the right to vote until they become such citizens.

Section 178. Residency, registration and poll tax requirements for electors.

To entitle a person to vote at any election by the people, he shall have resided in the State at least two years, in the county one year, and in the precinct or ward three months, immediately preceding the election at which he offers to vote, and he shall have been duly registered as an elector, and shall have paid on or before the first day of February next preceding the date of the election at which he offers to vote, all poll taxes due from him for the year nineteen hundred and one, and for each subsequent year; provided, that any elector who within three months next preceding the date of the election at which he offers to vote, has removed from one precinct or ward to another precinct or ward in the same county, incorporated town or city, shall have the right to vote in the precinct or ward from which he has so removed, if he would have been entitled to vote in such precinct or ward but for such removal.

Section 179. Method of voting.

All elections by the people shall be by ballot, and all elections by persons in a representative capacity shall be viva voce.

Section 180. Persons qualified to register as electors Prior to December 20, 1902.

The following male citizens of this State, who are citizens of the United States, and every male resident of foreign birth who, before the ratification of this Constitution, shall have legally declared his intention to become a citizen of the United States, and who shall not have had an opportunity to perfect his citizenship prior to the twentieth day of December, nineteen hundred and two, twenty-one years old or upwards, who, if their place of residence shall remain unchanged, will have, at the date of the next general election the qualifications as to residence prescribed in Section 178 of this Constitution, and who are not disqualified under Section 182 of this Constitution, shall, upon application, be entitled to register as electors prior to the twentieth day of December, nineteen hundred and two, namely:

First—All who have honorably served in the land or naval forces of the United States in the war of 1812, or in the war with Mexico, or in any war with the Indians, or in the war between the States, or in the war with Spain, or who honorably served in the land or naval forces of the Confederate States, or of the State of Alabama in the war between the States; or,

Second—The lawful descendants of persons who honorably served in the land or naval forces of the United States in the war of the American Revolution, or in the war of 1812, or in the war with Mexico, or in any war with the Indians, or in the war between the States, or in the land or naval forces of the Confederate States, or of the State of Alabama in the war between the States; or,

Third—All persons who are of good character and who understand the duties and obligations of citizenship under a republican form of government.

Section 181. Same After January 1, 1903.

After the first day of January, nineteen hundred and three, the following persons, and no others, who, if their place of residence shall remain unchanged, will have, at the date of the next general election, the qualifications as to residence prescribed in Section 178 of this article, shall be qualified to register as electors; provided, they shall not be disqualified under Section 182 of this Constitution.

First—Those who can read and write any article of the Constitution of the United States in the English language, and who are physically unable to work; and those who can read and write any article of the Constitution of the United States in the English language, and who have worked or been regularly engaged in some lawful employment, business or occupation, trade or calling for the greater part of the twelve months next preceding the time they offer to register; and those who are unable to read and write, if such inability is due solely to physical disability; or,

Second—The owner in good faith in his own right, or the husband of a woman who is the owner in good faith, in her own right, of forty acres of land situate in this State, upon which they reside; or the owner in good faith in his own right, or the husband of any woman who is the owner in good faith, in her own right, of real estate situate in this State, assessed for taxation at the value of three hundred dollars or more, or the owner in good faith, in his own right, or the husband of a woman who is the owner in good faith, in her own right, of personal property in this State assessed for taxation at three hundred dollars or more; provided, that the taxes due upon such real or personal property for the year next preceding the year in which he offers to register shall have been paid, unless the assessment shall have been legally contested and is undetermined.

Section 182. Certain persons disqualified from registering and voting.

The following persons shall be disqualified both from registering and from voting, namely:

All idiots and insane persons; those who shall by reason of conviction of crime be disqualified from voting at the time of the ratification of this Constitution; those who shall be convicted of treason, murder, arson, embezzlement, malfeasance in office, larceny, receiving stolen property, obtaining property or money under false pretenses, perjury, subornation of perjury, robbery, assault with intent to rob, burglary, forgery, bribery, assault and battery on the wife, bigamy, living in adultery, sodomy, incest, rape, miscegenation, crime against nature, or any crime punishable by imprisonment in the penitentiary, or of any infamous crime or crime involving moral turpitude; also, any person who shall be convicted as a vagrant or tramp, or of selling or offering to sell his vote or the vote of another, or of making or offering to make false return in any election by the people or in any primary election to procure the nomination or election of any person to any office, or of suborning any witness or registrar to secure the registration of any person as an elector.

Section 183. Qualifications as elector required to participate in primary elections, party conventions, mass meetings or other methods of political party action.

No person shall be qualified to vote, or participate in any primary election, party convention, mass meeting or other method of party action of any political party or faction, who shall not possess the qualifications prescribed in this article for an elector, or who shall be disqualified from voting under the provisions of this article.

Section 184. Applicability of article as to elections held after 1902 general election.

No person, not registered and qualified as an elector under the provisions of this article shall vote at the general election in nineteen hundred and two, or at any subsequent State, county or municipal election, general, local or special; but the provisions of this article shall not apply to any election held prior to the general election in the year nineteen hundred and two.

Section 185. Oath or affirmation when vote challenged; false oath or affirmation constitutes perjury.

Any elector whose right to vote shall be challenged for any legal cause before an election officer, shall be required to swear or affirm that the matter of the challenge is untrue before his vote shall be received, and any one who wilfully swears or affirms falsely thereto shall be guilty of perjury, and upon conviction thereof shall be imprisoned in the penitentiary for not less than one nor more than five years.

Section 186. Legislature to provide for registration procedure after January 1, 1903; procedure for registration prior to January 1, 1903.

The Legislature shall provide by law for the registration, after the first day of January, nineteen hundred and three, of all qualified electors. Until the first day of January, nineteen hundred and three, all electors shall be registered under and in accordance with the requirements of this section as follows:

First—Registration shall be conducted in each county by a board of three reputable and suitable persons resident in the county, who shall not hold any elective office during their term, to be appointed within sixty days after the ratification of this Constitution, by the Governor, Auditor and Commissioner of Agriculture and Industries, or by a majority of them acting as a board of appointment. If one or more of the persons appointed on such a board of registration shall refuse, neglect or be unable to qualify or serve, or if a vacancy or vacancies occur in the membership of the board of registrars from any cause, the Governor, Auditor and Commissioner of Agriculture and Industries, or a majority of them, acting as a board of appointment, shall make other appointments to fill such board. Each registrar shall receive two dollars per day, to be paid by the State, and disbursed by the several Judges of Probate, for each entire day's attendance upon the sessions of the board. Before entering upon the performance of the duties of his office, each registrar shall take the same oath required of the judicial officers of the State, which oath may be administered by any person authorized by law to administer oaths. The oath shall be in writing and subscribed by the registrar, and filed in the office of the Judge of Probate of the county.

Second—Prior to the first day of August, nineteen hundred and two, the Board of Registrars in each county shall visit each precinct at least once and oftener if necessary to make a complete registration of all persons entitled to register, and shall remain there at least one day from eight o'clock in the morning until sunset. They shall give at least twenty days' notice of the time when, and the place in the precinct where they will attend to register applicants for registration, by bills posted at five or more public places in each election precinct, and by advertisement once a week for three successive weeks in a newspaper, if there be one published in the county. Upon failure to give such notice, or to attend any appointment made by them in any precinct, they shall, after like notice, fill new appointments therein; but the time consumed by the board in completing such registration shall not exceed sixty working days in any county, except that in counties of more than nine hundred square miles in area, such board may consume seventy-five working days in completing the registration, and except that in counties in which there is any city of eight thousand or more inhabitants, the board may remain in session, in addition to the time hereinbefore prescribed, for not more than three successive weeks in each of such cities; and thereafter the board may sit from time to time in each of such cities not more than one week in each month, and except that in the county of Jefferson the board may hold an additional session of not exceeding five consecutive days duration for each session, in each town or city of more than one thousand and less than eight thousand inhabitants. No person shall be registered except at the county site or in the precinct in which he resides. The registrars shall issue to each person registered a certificate of registration.

Third—The Board of Registrars shall not register any person between the first day of August, nineteen hundred and two, and the Friday next preceding the day of election in November, nineteen hundred and two. On Friday and Saturday next preceding the day of election in November, nineteen hundred and two, they shall sit in the court house of each county during such days, and shall register all applicants having the qualifications prescribed by Section 180 of this Constitution, and not disqualified under Section 182, who shall have reached the age of twenty-one years after the first day of August, nineteen hundred and two, or who shall prove to the reasonable satisfaction of the board that, by reason of physical disability or unavoidable absence from the county, they had no opportunity to register prior to the first day of August, nineteen hundred and two, and they shall not on such days register any other persons. When there are two or more court houses in a county, the registrars may sit during such two days at the court house they may select, but shall give ten days' notice, by bills posted at each of the court houses, designating the court house at which they will sit.

Fourth—The Board of Registrars shall hold sessions at the court house of their respective counties during the entire third week in November, nineteen hundred and two, and for six working days next prior to the twentieth day of December, nineteen hundred and two, during which sessions they shall register all persons applying who possess the qualifications prescribed in Section 180 of this Constitution, and who shall not be disqualified under Section 182. In counties where there are two or more court houses the Board of Registrars shall divide the time equally between them. The Board of Registrars shall give notice of the time and place of such sessions by posting notices at each court house in their respective counties, and at each voting place and at three other public places in the county, and by publication once a week for two consecutive weeks in a newspaper, if one be published in the county; such notices to be posted and such publications to be commenced as early as practicable in the first week of November, nineteen hundred and two. Failure on the part of the registrars to conform to the provisions of this article as to the giving of the required notices shall not invalidate any registration made by them.

Fifth—The Board of Registrars shall have power to examine, under oath or affirmation, all applicants for registration, and to take testimony touching the qualifications of such applicants. Each member of such board is authorized to administer the oath to be taken by the applicants and witnesses, which shall be in the following form, and subscribed by the person making it, and preserved by the board, namely: "I solemnly swear (or affirm) that in the matter of the application of .... for registration as an elector, I will speak the truth, the whole truth, and nothing but the truth, so help me God." Any person who upon such examination makes any willfully false statement in reference to any material matter touching the qualification of any applicant for registration shall be guilty of perjury, and upon conviction thereof, shall be imprisoned in the penitentiary for not less than one nor more than five years.

Sixth—The action of the majority of the Board of Registrars shall be the action of the board, and a majority of the board shall constitute a quorum for the transaction of all business. Any person to whom registration is denied shall have the right of appeal, without giving security for costs, within thirty days after such denial, by filing a petition in the Circuit Court or court of like jurisdiction held for the county in which he seeks to register, to have his qualifications as an elector determined. Upon the filing of the petition the clerk of the court shall give notice thereof to any Solicitor authorized to represent the State in said county, whose duty it shall be to appear and defend against the petition on behalf of the State. Upon such trial the court shall charge the jury only as to what constitutes the qualifications that entitled the applicant to become an elector at the time he applied for registration, and the jury shall determine the weight and effect of the evidence and return a verdict. From the judgment rendered an appeal will lie to the Supreme Court in favor of the petitioner, to be taken within thirty days. Final judgment in favor of the petitioner shall entitle him to registration as of the date of his application to the registrars.

Seventh—The Secretary of State shall, at the expense of the State, have prepared and shall furnish to the registrars and judges of probate of the several counties a sufficient number of registration books and of blank forms of the oath, certificates of registration and notices required to be given by the registrars. The cost of the publication in newspapers of the notices required to be given by the registrars shall be paid by the State, the bills therefor to be rendered to the Secretary of State and approved by him.

Eighth—Any person who registers for another, or who registers more than once, and any registrar who enters the name of any person on the list of registered voters, without such person having made application in person under oath on a form provided for that purpose, or who knowingly registers any person more than once, or who knowingly enters a name upon the registration list as the name of a voter, without any one of that name applying to register, shall be guilty of a felony, and upon conviction thereof shall be imprisoned in the penitentiary for not less than one nor more than five years.

Section 187. County board of registrars to furnish list of registered voters to judges of probate by February 1, 1903; judges of probate to file list with secretary of state by March 1, 1903; term for which registration valid; certificate of registratio

The Board of Registrars in each county shall on or before the first day of February, nineteen hundred and three, or as soon thereafter as practicable, file in the office of the Judge of Probate in their county, a complete list sworn to by them of all persons registered in their county, showing the age of such persons so registered, with the precinct or ward in which each of such persons resides set opposite the name of such persons and shall also file a like list in the office of the Secretary of State. The Judge of Probate shall, on or before the first day of March, nineteen hundred and three, or as soon thereafter as practicable, cause to be made from such list in duplicate, in the books furnished by the Secretary of State, an alphabetical list by precincts of the persons shown by the list of the registrars to have been registered in the county, and shall file one of such alphabetical lists in the office of the Secretary of State; for which services by the Judges of Probate compensation shall be provided by the Legislature. The Judges of Probate shall keep both the original list filed by the registrars and the alphabetical list made therefrom as records in the office of the Judge of Probate of the county. Unless he shall become disqualified under the provisions of this article, any one who shall register prior to the first day of January, nineteen hundred and three, shall remain an elector during life, and shall not be required to register again unless he changes his residence, in which event he may register again on production of his certificate. The certificate of the registrars or of the Judge of Probate or of the Secretary of State shall be sufficient evidence to establish the fact of such life registration. Such certificate shall be issued free of charge to the elector, and the Legislature shall provide by law for the renewal of such certificate when lost, mutilated or destroyed.

Section 188. Certain information to be furnished prior to registration.

From and after the first day of January, nineteen hundred and three, any applicant for registration may be required to state under oath, to be administered by the registrar or by any person authorized by law to administer oaths, where he lived during the five years next preceding the time at which he applies to register, and the name or names by which he was known during that period, and the name of his employer or employers, if any, during such period. Any applicant for registration who refuses to state such facts, or any of them, shall not be entitled to register, and any person so offering to register, who wilfully makes a false statement in regard to such matters, or any of them, shall be guilty of perjury, and upon conviction thereof shall be imprisoned in the penitentiary for not less than one nor more than five years.

Section 189. Testimony may be required of any person other than defendant in trials of contested elections, proceedings to investigate elections and criminal prosecutions under election laws; immunity from prosecution due to testimony given.

In the trial of any contested election, and in proceedings to investigate any election, and in criminal prosecutions for violations of the election laws, no person other than a defendant in such criminal prosecutions shall be allowed to withhold his testimony on the ground that he may criminate himself or subject himself to public infamy; but such person shall not be prosecuted for any offense arising out of the transactions concerning which he testified, but may be prosecuted for perjury committed on such examination.

Section 190. Duty of Legislature to pass laws regulating elections, primary elections and purging of registration lists.

The Legislature shall pass laws not inconsistent with this Constitution to regulate and govern elections, and all such laws shall be uniform throughout the State; and shall provide by law for the manner of holding elections and of ascertaining the result of the same, and shall provide general registration laws not inconsistent with the provisions of this article, for the registration of all qualified electors from and after the first day of January, nineteen hundred and three. The Legislature shall also make provision by law, not inconsistent with this article, for the regulation of primary elections, and for punishing frauds at the same, but shall not make primary elections compulsory. The Legislature shall by law provide for purging the registration list of the names of those who die, become insane, or convicted of crime, or otherwise disqualified as electors under the provisions of this Constitution, and of any names which may have been fraudulently entered on such list by the registrars; provided, that a trial by jury may be had on the demand of any person whose name is proposed to be stricken from the list.

Section 191. Protection against evils of intoxicating liquors at elections.

It shall be the duty of the Legislature to pass adequate laws giving protection against the evils arising from the use of intoxicating liquors at all elections.

Section 192. Electors immune from arrest going to, attending and returning from elections.

Electors shall in all cases, except treason, felony or breach of the peace, be privileged from arrest during their attendance at elections, or while going to or returning therefrom.

Section 193. Returns of elections for certain officials to be made to secretary of state.

Returns of elections for members of the Legislature and for all civil officers who are to be commissioned by the Governor, except the Attorney General, State Auditor, Secretary of State, State Treasurer, Superintendent of Education, and Commissioner of Agriculture and Industries, shall be made to the Secretary of State.

Section 194. Poll tax Amount; maximum age for payment; when due and payable; when delinquent; returns of collections to be separate from other collections.

The poll tax mentioned in this article shall be one dollar and fifty cents upon each male inhabitant of the State, over the age of twenty-one years, and under the age of forty-five years, who would not now be exempt by law; but the Legislature is authorized to increase the maximum age fixed in this section to not more than sixty years. Such poll tax shall become due and payable on the first day of October in each year, and become delinquent on the first day of the next succeeding February, but no legal process, nor any fee or commission shall be allowed for the collection thereof. The Tax Collector shall make returns of poll tax collections separate from other collections.

Section 195. Same Payment of tax of another; advance of money for payment in order to influence vote.

Any person who shall pay the poll tax of another, or advance him money for that purpose in order to influence his vote, shall be guilty of bribery, and upon conviction therefor shall be imprisoned in the penitentiary for not less than one nor more than five years.

Section 196. Severability of article.

If any section or subdivision of this article shall, for any reason, be or be held by any court of competent jurisdiction and of final resort, to be invalid, inoperative or void, the residue of this article shall not be thereby invalidated or affected.

Article IX: Representation

Section 197. Ratio of senators to representatives.

The whole number of Senators shall be not less than one-fourth or more than one-third of the whole number of Representatives.

Section 198. Maximum number of members of House of Representatives; apportionment of house based on decennial census of United States.

The House of Representatives shall consist of not more than one hundred and five members, unless new counties shall be created, in which event each new county shall be entitled to one Representative. The members of the House of Representatives shall be apportioned by the Legislature among the several counties of the State, according to the number of inhabitants in them respectively, as ascertained by the decennial census of the United States, which apportionment when made shall not be subject to alteration until the next session of the Legislature after the next decennial census of the United States shall have been taken.

Section 199. Duty of Legislature to fix number of representatives and apportion them among counties following each decennial census; each county entitled to at least one representative.

It shall be the duty of the Legislature at its first session after the taking of the decennial census of the United States in the year nineteen hundred and ten, and after each subsequent decennial census, to fix by law the number of Representatives and apportion them among the several counties of the State, according to the number of inhabitants in them respectively; provided, that each county shall be entitled to at least one Representative.

Section 200. Duty of Legislature to fix number of senators and divide state into senatorial districts; equality of senatorial districts; senatorial districts not to be changed until next apportioning session; division of counties between senatorial dist

It shall be the duty of the Legislature at its first session after taking of the decennial census of the United States in the year nineteen hundred and ten, and after each subsequent decennial census, to fix by law the number of Senators, and to divide the State into as many Senatorial districts as there are Senators, which districts shall be as nearly equal to each other in the number of inhabitants as may be, and each shall be entitled to one Senator, and no more; and such districts when formed, shall not be changed until the next apportioning session of the Legislature, after the next decennial census of the United States shall have been taken; provided, that counties created after the next preceding apportioning session of the Legislature may be attached to Senatorial districts. No county shall be divided between two districts, and no district shall be made up of two or more counties not contiguous to each other.

Section 201. State may provide for enumeration of inhabitants for purpose of apportionment of representatives and senators.

Should any decennial census of the United States not be taken, or if when taken the same, as to this State be not full and satisfactory, the Legislature shall have the power at its first session after the time shall have elapsed for the taking of said census, to provide for an enumeration of all the inhabitants of this State, upon which it shall be the duty of the Legislature to make the apportionment of Representatives and Senators as provided for in this article.

Section 202. Initial apportionment of house of representatives.

Until the Legislature shall make an apportionment of Representatives among the several counties, as provided in the preceding section, the counties of Autauga, Baldwin, Bibb, Blount, Cherokee, Chilton, Choctaw, Clay, Cleburne, Coffee, Colbert, Conecuh, Coosa, Covington, Crenshaw, Cullman, Dale, DeKalb, Escambia, Fayette, Franklin, Geneva, Greene, Lamar, Lawrence, Limestone, Macon, Marion, Marshall, Monroe, Pickens, Randolph, St. Clair, Shelby, Washington, and Winston, shall each have one Representative; the counties of Barbour, Bullock, Butler, Calhoun, Chambers, Clarke, Elmore, Etowah, Hale, Henry, Jackson, Lauderdale, Lee, Lowndes, Madison, Marengo, Morgan, Perry, Pike, Russell, Sumter, Talladega, Tallapoosa, Tuscaloosa, Walker, and Wilcox, shall each have two Representatives; the counties of Dallas and Mobile shall each have three Representatives; the county of Montgomery shall have four Representatives; and the county of Jefferson shall have seven Representatives.

Section 203. Initial apportionment of senatorial districts.

Until the Legislature shall divide the State into Senatorial districts, as herein provided, the Senatorial districts shall be as follows:

First district, Lauderdale and Limestone;

Second district, Lawrence and Morgan;

Third district, Blount, Cullman and Winston;

Fourth district, Madison;

Fifth district, Jackson and Marshall;

Sixth district, Etowah and St. Clair;

Seventh district, Calhoun;

Eighth district, Talladega;

Ninth district, Chambers and Randolph;

Tenth district, Tallapoosa and Elmore;

Eleventh district, Tuscaloosa;

Twelfth district, Fayette, Lamar and Walker;

Thirteenth district, Jefferson;

Fourteenth district, Pickens and Sumter;

Fifteenth district, Autauga, Chilton and Shelby;

Sixteenth district, Lowndes;

Seventeenth district, Butler, Conecuh and Covington;

Eighteenth district, Bibb and Perry;

Nineteenth district, Choctaw, Clarke and Washington;

Twentieth district, Marengo;

Twenty-first district, Baldwin, Escambia and Monroe;

Twenty-second district, Wilcox;

Twenty-third district, Dale and Geneva;

Twenty-fourth district, Barbour;

Twenty-fifth district, Coffee, Crenshaw and Pike;

Twenty-sixth district, Bullock and Macon;

Twenty-seventh district, Lee and Russell;

Twenty-eighth district, Montgomery;

Twenty-ninth district, Cherokee and DeKalb;

Thirtieth district, Dallas;

Thirty-first district, Colbert, Franklin and Marion;

Thirty-second district, Greene and Hale;

Thirty-third district, Mobile;

Thirty-fourth district, Cleburne, Clay and Coosa;

Thirty-fifth district, Henry.

Article X: Exemptions

Section 204. Personal property of value of one thousand dollars exempt from sale, execution or other process of court issued for collection of debt.

The personal property of any resident of this State to the value of one thousand dollars, to be selected by such resident, shall be exempt from sale on execution or other process of any court, issued for the collection of any debt contracted since the thirteenth day of July, eighteen hundred and sixty-eight, or after the ratification of this Constitution.

Section 205. Homestead not exceeding eighty acres or city, town or village lot not exceeding two thousand dollars in value exempt from sale, execution or other process of court issued for collection of debt; exception as to mortgages.

Every homestead, not exceeding eighty acres, and the dwelling and appurtenances thereon, to be selected by the owner thereof, and not in any city, town or village, or in lieu thereof, at the option of the owner, any lot in a city, town or village, with the dwelling and appurtenances thereon owned and occupied by any resident of this State, and not exceeding the value of two thousand dollars, shall be exempt from sale on execution or any other process from a court; for any debt contracted since the thirteenth day of July, eighteen hundred and sixty-eight, or after the ratification of this Constitution. Such exemption, however, shall not extend to any mortgage lawfully obtained, but such mortgage or other alienation of said homestead by the owner thereof, if a married man, shall not be valid without the voluntary signature and assent of the wife to the same.

Section 206. Homestead of family exempt from payments of debt after death of owner during minority of children.

The homestead of a family, after the death of the owner thereof, shall be exempt from the payment of any debts contracted since the thirteenth day of July, eighteen hundred and sixty-eight, or after the ratification of this Constitution, in all cases, during the minority of the children.

Section 207. Laborers' liens and mechanics' liens not barred by sections 204 and 205.

The provisions of Sections 204 and 205 of this Constitution shall not be so construed as to prevent a laborers' lien for work done and performed for the person claiming such exemption, or a mechanics' lien for work done on the premises.

Section 208. Homestead exempt upon death of owner, leaving widow, but no children.

If the owner of a homestead die, leaving a widow, but no children, such homestead shall be exempt, and the rents and profits thereof shall inure to her benefit.

Section 209. Property rights of females; property of wife not liable for debts, etc., of husband.

The real and personal property of any female in this State, acquired before marriage, and all property, real and personal, to which she may afterwards be entitled by gift, grant, inheritance or devise, shall be and remain the separate estate and property of such female, and shall not be liable for any debts, obligations or engagements of her husband, and may be devised or bequeathed by her, the same as if she were a feme sole.

Section 210. Waiver of right of exemption.

The right of exemption hereinbefore secured may be waived by an instrument in writing, and when such waiver relates to realty, the instrument must be signed by both the husband and the wife, and attested by one witness.

Article XI: Taxation

Section 211. Property taxes to be assessed in exact proportion to value of property.

All taxes levied on property in this State shall be assessed in exact proportion to the value of such property, but no tax shall be assessed upon any debt for rent or hire of real or personal property, while owned by the landlord or hirer during the current year of such rental or hire, if such real or personal property be assessed at its full value.

Section 212. Power to levy taxes not to be delegated.

The power to levy taxes shall not be delegated to individuals or private corporations or associations.

Section 213. Creation of state debt after ratification of Constitution; temporary loans; refunding bonds for existing indebtedness.

After the ratification of this Constitution, no new debt shall be created against, or incurred by this State, or its authority, except to repel invasion or suppress insurrection, and then only by a concurrence of two-thirds of the members of each House of the Legislature, and the vote shall be taken by yeas and nays and entered on the Journals; and any act creating or incurring any new debt against this State, except as herein provided for, shall be absolutely void; provided, the Governor may be authorized to negotiate temporary loans, never to exceed three hundred thousand dollars, to meet the deficiencies in the treasury, and until the same is paid no new loan shall be negotiated; provided further, that this section shall not be so construed as to prevent the issuance of bonds for the purpose of refunding the existing bonded indebtedness of the State.

Section 214. Limitation on state property tax rate.

The Legislature shall not have the power to levy in any one year a greater rate of taxation than sixty-five one-hundredths of one per centum on the value of the taxable property within this State.

Section 215. Limitation on county property tax rates; special county taxes for public buildings, bridges and roads.

No county in this State shall be authorized to levy a greater rate of taxation in any one year on the value of the taxable property therein than one-half of one per centum; provided, that to pay debts existing on the sixth day of December, eighteen hundred and seventy-five, an additional rate of one-fourth of one per centum may be levied and collected which shall be appropriated exclusively to the payment of such debts and the interest thereon; provided further, that to pay any debt or liability now existing against any county, incurred for the erection, construction, or maintenance of the necessary public buildings or bridges, or that may hereafter be created for the erection of necessary public buildings, bridges or roads, any county may levy and collect such special taxes, not to exceed one-fourth of one per centum, as may have been or may hereafter be authorized by law, which taxes so levied and collected shall be applied exclusively to the purposes for which the same were so levied and collected.

Section 216. Limitation on property tax rates of municipal corporations.

No city, town, village or other municipal corporation, other than as provided in this article, shall levy or collect a higher rate of taxation in any one year on the property situated therein than one-half of one per centum of the value of such property as assessed for State taxation during the preceding year; provided, that for the purpose of paying debts existing on the sixth day of

December, eighteen hundred and seventy-five, and the interest thereon, a tax of one per centum may be levied and collected, to be applied exclusively to the payment of such indebtedness; and provided further, that this section shall not apply to the city of Mobile, which city may from and after the ratification of this Constitution, levy a tax not to exceed the rate of three-fourths of one per centum to pay the expenses of the city government, and may also levy a tax not to exceed three-fourths of one per centum to pay the debt existing on the sixth day of December, eighteen hundred and seventy-five, with interest thereon, or any renewal of such debt; and, provided further, that this section shall not apply to the cities of Birmingham, Huntsville and Bessemer, and the town of Andalusia, which cities and town may levy and collect a tax not to exceed one-half of one per centum in addition to the tax of one-half of one per centum as hereinbefore allowed to be levied and collected, such special tax to be applied exclusively to the payment of interest on bonds of said cities of Birmingham, Huntsville and Bessemer and town of Andalusia, respectively, heretofore issued in pursuance of law, or now authorized by law to be issued, and for a sinking fund to pay off said bonds at the maturity thereof; and provided further, that this section shall not apply to the city of Montgomery, which city shall have the right to levy and collect a tax of not exceeding one-half of one per centum per annum upon the value of the taxable property therein, as fixed for State taxation, for general purposes, and an additional tax of not exceeding three-fourths of one per centum per annum upon the value of the property therein, as fixed for State taxation, to be devoted exclusively to the payment of its public debt, interest thereon, and renewals thereof, and to the maintenance of its public schools, and public conveniences; and provided further, that this section shall not apply to Troy, Attalla, Gadsden, Woodlawn, Brewton, Pratt City, Ensley, Wylam, and Avondale, which cities and towns may from and after the ratification of this Constitution, levy and collect an additional tax of not exceeding one-half of one per centum; and provided further, that this section shall not apply to the cities of Decatur, New Decatur and Cullman, which cities may from and after the ratification of this Constitution, levy and collect an additional tax of not exceeding three-tenths of one per centum per annum; such special tax of said city of Decatur to be applied exclusively for the public schools, public school buildings, and public improvements; and such special tax of New Decatur and Cullman to be applied exclusively for educational purposes, and to be expended under their respective boards of Public School Trustees; but this additional tax shall not be levied by Troy, Attalla, Gadsden, Woodlawn, Brewton, Pratt City, Ensley, Wylam, Avondale, Decatur, New Decatur, or Cullman unless authorized by a majority vote of the qualified electors voting at a special election held for the purpose of ascertaining whether or not said tax shall be levied; and provided further, that the purposes for which such special tax is sought to be levied shall be stated in such election call, and, if authorized, the revenue derived from such special tax shall be used for no other purpose than that stated; and provided further, that the additional tax authorized to be levied by the city of Troy, when so levied and collected, shall be used exclusively in the payment of the bonds and interest coupons thereon, hereafter issued in the adjustment of the present bonded indebtedness of said city; and provided further, that the additional tax authorized to be levied and collected by the city of Attalla shall, when so levied and collected, be used exclusively in the payment of bonds to the amount of not exceeding twenty-five thousand dollars, and the interest coupons thereon, hereafter to be issued in the adjustment of the present indebtedness of said city; provided further, that the governing boards of said cities, which are authorized to levy an additional tax after the holding of an election as aforesaid, are hereby authorized to provide by ordinance the necessary machinery for the holding of said election and declaring the result thereof.

Section 217. Property of private corporations, associations and individuals to be taxed at same rate; exception as to religious, educational and charitable property.

The property of private corporations, associations and individuals of this State shall forever be taxed at the same rate; provided, this section shall not apply to institutions devoted exclusively to religious, educational or charitable purposes.

Section 218. Counties and municipal corporations exempt from payment of charges payable from state treasury.

The Legislature shall not have the power to require counties or other municipal corporations to pay any charges which are now payable out of the State treasury.

Section 219 Estate taxes.

The Legislature may levy a tax of not more than two and one-half per centum of the value of all estates, real and personal, money, public and private securities of every kind in this State, passing from any person who may die seized and possessed thereof, or of any part of such estate, money or securities, or interest therein, transferred by the intestate laws of this State, or by will, deed, grant, bargain, sale or gift, made or intended to take effect in possession after death of the grantor, devisor, or donor, to any person or persons, bodies politic or corporate, in trust or otherwise, other than to or for the use of the father, mother, husband, wife, brothers, sisters, children or lineal descendants of the grantor, devisor, donor or intestate.

Article XII: Corporations

Article Municipal Corporations

Section 220. Consent of municipal corporation prerequisite to use of public property for public utility or private enterprise purposes.

No person, firm, association or corporation shall be authorized or permitted to use the streets, avenues, alleys or public places of any city, town or village for the construction or operation of any public utility or private enterprise, without first obtaining the consent of the proper authorities of such city, town or village.

Section 221. Payment of state license tax, etc., not to excuse payment of other privilege and license taxes.

The Legislature shall not enact any law which will permit any person, firm, corporation or association to pay a privilege, license or other tax to the State of Alabama, and relieve him or it from the payment of all other privilege and license taxes in the State.

Section 222. Issuance of bonds by counties, municipal corporations, districts and other political subdivisions of counties.

The Legislature, after the ratification of this Constitution, shall have authority to pass general laws authorizing the counties, cities, towns, villages, districts or other political subdivisions of counties to issue bonds, but no bonds shall be issued under authority of a general law unless such issue of bonds be first authorized by a majority vote by ballot of the qualified voters of such county, city, town, village, district, or other political subdivision of a county, voting upon such proposition. The ballot used at such election shall contain the words "For ... bond issue," and "Against ... bond issue," (the character of the bond to be shown in the blank space), and the voter shall indicate his choice by placing a cross mark before or after the one or the other. This section shall not apply to the renewal, refunding or reissue of bonds lawfully issued, nor to the issuance of bonds in cases where the same have been authorized by laws enacted prior to the ratification of this Constitution, nor shall this section apply to obligations incurred or bonds to be issued to procure means to pay for street and sidewalk improvements or sanitary or storm water sewers, the cost of which is to be assessed, in whole or in part, against the property abutting said improvements or drained by such sanitary or storm water sewers.

Section 223. Limitation on assessments for public improvements by municipal corporations.

No city, town or other municipality shall make any assessment for the cost of sidewalks or street paving, or for the cost of the construction of any sewers against property abutting on such street or sidewalk so paved, or drained by such sewers, in excess of the increased value of such property by reason of the special benefits derived from such improvements.

Section 224. Limitation on county indebtedness.

No county shall become indebted in an amount including present indebtedness, greater than three and one-half per centum of the assessed value of the property therein; provided, this limitation shall not affect any existing indebtedness in excess of such three and one-half per centum, which has already been created or authorized by existing law to be created; provided, that any county which has already incurred a debt exceeding three and one-half per centum of the assessed value of the property therein, shall be authorized to incur an indebtedness of one and a half per centum of the assessed value of such property in addition to the debt already existing. Nothing herein contained shall prevent any county from issuing bonds, or other obligations, to fund or refund any indebtedness now existing or authorized by existing laws to be created.

Section 225. Indebtedness of municipal corporations Limitation; exception as to Sheffield and Tuscumbia.

No city, town or other municipal corporation having a population of less than six thousand, except as hereafter provided, shall become indebted in an amount, including present indebtedness, exceeding five per centum of the assessed value of the property therein, except for the construction of or purchase of water works, gas or electric lighting plants, or sewerage, or for the improvement of streets, for which purposes an additional indebtedness not exceeding three per centum may be created; provided, this limitation shall not affect any debt now authorized by law to be created, nor any temporary loans to be paid within one year, made in anticipation of the collection of taxes, not exceeding one-fourth of the annual revenues of such city or town. All towns and cities having a population of six thousand or more, also Gadsden, Ensley, Decatur, and New Decatur, are hereby authorized to become indebted in an amount including present indebtedness, not exceeding seven per centum of the assessed valuation of the property therein, provided that there shall not be included in the limitation of the indebtedness of such last described cities and towns the following classes of indebtedness, to-wit: Temporary loans, to be paid within one year, made in anticipation of the collection of taxes, and not exceeding one-fourth of the general revenues, bonds or other obligations already issued, or which may hereafter be issued for the purpose of acquiring, providing or constructing school houses, water works and sewers; and obligations incurred and bonds issued for street or sidewalk improvements, where the cost of the same, in whole or in part, is to be assessed against the property abutting said improvements; provided, that the proceeds of all obligations issued as herein provided, in excess of said seven per centum shall not be used for any purpose other than that for which said obligations were issued. Nothing contained in this article shall prevent the funding or refunding of existing indebtedness. This section shall not apply to the cities of Sheffield and Tuscumbia.

Section 226. Same Municipal corporations whose present indebtedness exceeds constitutional limitation; exception as to Sheffield and Tuscumbia.

No city, town or village, whose present indebtedness exceeds the limitation imposed by this Constitution, shall be allowed to become indebted in any further amount, except as otherwise provided in this Constitution, until such indebtedness shall be reduced within such limit; provided, however, that nothing herein contained shall prevent any municipality, except the city of Gadsden, from issuing bonds already authorized by law; provided further, that this section shall not apply to the cities of Sheffield and Tuscumbia.

Section 227. Liability of public utilities in municipal corporations for damages to abutting property owners.

Any person, firm, association or corporation, who may construct or operate any public utility along or across the public streets of any city, town or village, under any privilege or franchise permitting such construction or operation, shall be liable to abutting proprietors for the actual damage done to the abutting property on account of such construction or operation.

Section 228. Maximum term of public utility franchises in cities and towns having population of six thousand or more.

No city or town having a population of more than six thousand shall have authority to grant to any person, firm, corporation or association the right to use its streets, avenues, alleys, or public places for the construction or operation of water works, gas works, telephone or telegraph line, electric light or power plants, steam or other heating plants, street railroads, or any other public utility, except railroads other than street railroads for a longer period than thirty years.

Article Private Corporations

Section 229. Special laws conferring corporate powers prohibited; general law as to grant or amendment of corporate charters; corporation franchise taxes to be paid; exemption of benevolent, educational or religious corporations from franchise taxes.

The Legislature shall pass no special act conferring corporate powers, but it shall pass general laws under which corporations may be organized and corporate powers obtained, subject, nevertheless, to repeal at the will of the Legislature; and shall pass general laws under which charters may be altered or amended. The Legislature shall, by general law, provide for the payment to the State of Alabama of a franchise tax by corporations organized under the laws of this State, which shall be in proportion to the amount of capital stock; but strictly benevolent, educational or religious corporations shall not be required to pay such a tax. The charter of any corporation shall be subject to amendment, alteration or repeal under general laws.

Section 230. Cancellation of certain corporate charters.

All existing charters, under which a bona fide organization shall not have taken place and business commenced in good faith within twelve months from the time of the ratification of this Constitution, shall thereafter have no validity.

Section 231. Limitation on remitting forfeiture of corporate charters.

The Legislature shall not remit the forfeiture of the charter of any corporation now existing or alter or amend the same, nor pass any general or special law for the benefit of such corporation, other than in execution of a trust created by law or by contract, except upon condition that such corporation shall thereafter hold its charter subject to the provisions of this Constitution.

Section 232. Foreign corporations doing business in state.

No foreign corporation shall do any business in this State without having at least one known place of business and an authorized agent or agents therein, and without filing with the Secretary of State a certified copy of its articles of incorporation or association. Such corporation may be sued in any county where it does business, by service of process upon an agent anywhere in the State. The Legislature shall, by general law, provide for the payment to the State of Alabama of a franchise tax by such corporation, but such franchise tax shall be based on the actual amount of capital employed in this State. Strictly benevolent, educational or religious corporations shall not be required to pay such a tax.

Section 233. Corporations restricted to business authorized by charter.

No corporation shall engage in any business other than that expressly authorized in its charter or articles of incorporation.

Section 234. Restrictions on issuance of corporate stock and bonds.

No corporation shall issue stocks or bonds except for money, labor done, or property actually received; and all fictitious increase of stock or indebtedness shall be void. The stock and bonded indebtedness of corporations shall not be increased except in pursuance of general laws, nor without the consent of the persons holding the larger amount in value of stock, first obtained at a meeting to be held after thirty days' notice, given in pursuance of law.

Section 235. Taking of property for public use by municipal and other corporations.

Municipal and other corporations and individuals invested with the privilege of taking property for public use, shall make just compensation, to be ascertained as may be provided by law, for the property taken, injured or destroyed by the construction or enlargement of its works, highways or improvements, which compensation shall be paid before such taking, injury or destruction. The Legislature is hereby prohibited from denying the right of appeal from any preliminary assessment of damages against any such corporations or individuals made by viewers or otherwise, but such appeal shall not deprive those who have obtained the judgment of condemnation from a right of entry, provided the amount of damages assessed shall have been paid in the court in money, and a bond shall have been given in not less than double the amount of the damages assessed, with good and sufficient sureties, to pay such damages as the property owner may sustain; and the amount of damages in all cases of appeals shall on demand of either party, be determined by a jury according to law.

Section 236. Security for dues from private corporations; liability of stockholders.

Dues from private corporations shall be secured by such means as may be prescribed by law; but in no case shall any stockholder be individually liable otherwise than for the unpaid stock owned by him or her.

Section 237. Issuance of preferred stock by corporations.

No corporation shall issue preferred stock without the consent of the owners of two-thirds of the stock of said corporation.

Section 238. Authority of legislature to revoke charters of incorporation.

The legislature shall have the power to alter, amend, or revoke any charter of incorporation now existing and revocable at the ratification of this Constitution, or any that may be hereafter created, whenever, in its opinion, such charter may be injurious to the citizens of this state, in such manner, however, that no injustice shall be done to the stockholders.

Section 239. Telegraph and telephone companies.

Any association or corporation organized for the purpose, or any individual, shall have the right to construct and maintain lines of telegraph and telephone within this state, and connect the same with other lines; and the legislature shall, by general law of uniform operation, provide reasonable regulations to give full effect to this section. No telegraph or telephone company shall consolidate with or hold a controlling interest in the stock or bonds of any other telegraph or telephone company owning a complete line, or acquire, by purchase or otherwise, any other competing line of telegraph or telephone.

Section 240. Corporations may sue and be sued like natural persons.

All corporations shall have the right to sue, and shall be subject to be sued, in all courts in like cases as natural persons.

Section 241. "Corporation" defined.

The term "corporation," as used in this article shall be construed to include all joint stock companies, and all associations having any of the powers or privileges of corporations, not possessed by individuals or partnerships.

Railroads and Canals

Section 242. When railroads and canals deemed public highways; railroad and canal companies; common carriers; rights of railroad companies generally.

All railroads and canals not constructed and used exclusively for private purposes, shall be public highways, and all railroad and canal companies shall be common carriers. Any association or corporation organized for the purpose shall have the right to construct and operate a railway between any points in this state, and connect at the state line, with railroads of other states. Every railroad company shall have the right with its road to intersect, connect with, or cross any other railroad, and each shall receive and transport the freight, passengers, and cars, loaded or empty, of the others, without delay or discrimination.

Section 243. Regulation of railroad companies vested in legislature.

The power and authority of regulating railroad freight and passenger tariffs, the locating and building of passenger and freight depots, correcting abuses, preventing unjust discrimination and extortion and requiring reasonable and just rates of freight and passenger tariffs, are hereby conferred upon the legislature, whose duty it shall be to pass laws from time to time regulating freight and passenger tariffs, to prohibit unjust discrimination on the various railroads, canals, and rivers of the state, and to prohibit the charging of other than just and reasonable rates and enforce the same by adequate penalties.

Section 244. Giving free passes or discount tickets to members of Legislature or officers exercising judicial functions.

No railroad or other transportation company or corporation shall grant free passes or sell tickets or passes at a discount, other than as sold to the public generally, to any member of the legislature or to any officer exercising judicial functions under the laws of this State; and any such member or officer receiving such a pass or ticket for himself, or procuring the same for another, shall be guilty of a misdemeanor, and, upon conviction, shall be fined not exceeding five hundred dollars, and at the discretion of the court trying the case, in addition to such fine, may imprison for a term not exceeding six months, and upon conviction, shall be subject to impeachment and removal from office. The courts having jurisdiction shall give this law specially in charge to the Grand Juries, and when the evidence is sufficient to authorize an indictment, the Grand Jury must present a true bill. The Circuit Court or any other court of like jurisdiction in any county into or through which such member or officer is transported by the use of such prohibited pass or ticket, shall have jurisdiction of the case, provided only one prosecution shall be had for the same offense; and provided further, that the trial and judgment for one offense shall not bar a prosecution for another offense when the same pass or ticket is used; and provided further, that nothing herein shall prevent a member of the Legislature who is a bona fide employee of a railroad or other transportation company or corporation at the time of his election, from accepting or procuring for himself or another, not a member of the Legislature, or officer exercising judicial functions, a free pass over the railroads or other transportation company or corporation by which he is employed.

Section 245. Railroad companies not to give rebates or bonuses in nature thereof; deceiving or misleading public as to rates.

No railroad company shall give or pay any rebate, or a bonus in the nature thereof, directly or indirectly, or do any act to mislead or deceive the public as to the real rates charged or received for freights or passage; and any such payments shall be illegal and void, and these prohibitions shall be enforced by suitable penalties.

Section 246. Acceptance of article prerequisite to benefits of future legislation.

No railroad, canal or transportation company in existence at the time of the ratification of this Constitution, shall have the benefit of any future legislation by general or special laws other than in execution of a trust created by law or by contract, except on the condition of complete acceptance of all the provisions of this article.

Article XIII: Banks and Banking

Section 247. Authority of Legislature restricted.

The Legislature shall not have the power to establish or incorporate any bank or banking company or moneyed institution for the purpose of issuing bills of credit or bills payable to order or bearer, except under the conditions prescribed in this Constitution.

Section 248. Banking laws to be general; specie basis; authority of banks to issue bills to circulate as money.

No bank shall be established otherwise than under a general banking law, nor other than upon a specie basis; provided, that any bank may be established with authority to issue bills to circulate as money in an amount equal to the face value of bonds of the United States, or of this State, convertible into specie at their face value, which shall, before such bank is authorized to issue its bills for circulation, be deposited with the State Treasurer or other depository prescribed by law, in an amount equal to the aggregate of such proposed issue, with power in such treasurer or depository to dispose of any or all of such bonds for a sufficient amount of specie to redeem the circulating notes of such bank at any time and without delay, should such bank suspend specie payment or fail to redeem its notes on demand.

Section 249. Bills or notes issued as money redeemable in gold or silver; laws not to sanction suspension of specie payments.

All bills or notes issued as money shall be at all times redeemable in gold or silver, and no law shall be passed sanctioning directly or indirectly, the suspension by any bank or banking company of specie payment.

Section 250. Preference of certain creditors in case of insolvency of bank.

Holders of bank notes, and depositors who have not stipulated for interest, shall, for such notes and deposits, be entitled in case of insolvency, to preference of payment over all other creditors; provided, this section shall apply to all banks whether incorporated or not.

Section 251. Termination of business.

Every bank or banking company shall be required to cease all banking operations within twenty years from the time of its organization, unless the time be extended by law, and promptly thereafter close its business; but after it has closed its business it shall have corporate capacity to sue and shall be liable to suits until its affairs and liabilities are fully closed.

Section 252. Maximum rate of interest.

No bank shall receive, directly or indirectly, a greater rate of interest than shall be allowed by law to individuals for lending money.

Section 253. State and political subdivisions thereof not to be stockholders in banks or lend credit thereto.

Neither the State nor any political subdivision thereof, shall be a stockholder in any bank, nor shall the credit of the State or any political subdivision thereof be given or lent to any banking company, association or corporation.

Section 254. Examination of banks by public officers; semiannual reports by banks.

The Legislature shall by appropriate laws provide for the examination, by some public officer, of all banks and banking institutions and trust companies engaged in banking business in this State; and each of such banks and banking companies or institutions shall, through its president, or such other officer as the Legislature may designate, make a report under oath of its resources and liabilities at least twice a year.

Section 255. Applicability of article.

The provisions of this article shall apply to all banks except National banks, and to all trust companies and individuals doing a banking business, whether incorporated or not.

Article XIV: Education

Section 256. Duty of legislature to establish and maintain public school system; apportionment of public school fund; separate schools for white and colored children.

The Legislature shall establish, organize and maintain a liberal system of public school throughout the State for the benefit of the children thereof between the ages of seven and twenty-one years. The public school fund shall be apportioned to the several counties in proportion to the number of school children of school age therein, and shall be so apportioned to the schools in the districts or townships in the counties as to provide, as nearly as practicable, school terms of equal duration in such school districts or townships. Separate schools shall be provided for white and colored children, and no child of either race shall be permitted to attend a school of the other race.

Section 257. Principal from sale, etc., of school property to be preserved; disposition of income therefrom. Section 258 Property donated or appropriated for educational purposes and estates of persons dying without will or heirs to be applied to maintenance of public schools.

The principal of all funds arising from the sale or other disposition of lands or other property, which has been or may hereafter be granted or entrusted to this State or given by the United States for educational purposes, shall be preserved inviolate and undiminished; and the income arising therefrom shall be faithfully applied to the specific object of the original grants or appropriations.

Section 258. Property donated or appropriated for educational purposes and estates of persons dying without will or heirs to be applied to maintenance of public schools.

All lands or other property given by individuals, or appropriated by the State for educational purposes, and all estates of deceased persons who die without leaving a will or heir shall be faithfully applied to the maintenance of the public schools.

Section 259. Use of poll taxes for support of public schools.

All poll taxes collected in this State shall be applied to the support of the public schools in the respective counties where collected.

Section 260. Certain income to be applied to support and maintenance of public schools; special annual tax for schools; maximum annual levy on taxable property; priority for payment of bonded indebtedness of state.

The income arising from the Sixteenth Section trust fund, the surplus revenue fund, until it is called for by the United States government, and the funds enumerated in Sections 257 and 258 of this Constitution, together with a special annual tax of thirty cents on each one hundred dollars of taxable property in this State, which the Legislature shall levy, shall be applied to the support and maintenance of the public schools, and it shall be the duty of the Legislature to increase the public school fund from time to time as the necessity therefor and the condition of the treasury and the resources of the State may justify; provided, that nothing herein contained shall be so construed as to authorize the Legislature to levy in any one year a greater rate of State taxation for all purposes including schools than sixty-five cents on each one hundred dollars worth of taxable property; and provided further, that nothing herein contained shall prevent the Legislature from first providing for the payment of the bonded indebtedness of the State and interest thereon out of all the revenues of the State.

Section 261. Percentage of school funds for teachers' salaries.

Not more than four per cent. of all moneys raised or which may hereafter be appropriated for the support of public schools, shall be used or expended otherwise than for the payment of teachers employed in such schools; provided, that the Legislature may, by a vote of two-thirds of each House, suspend the operation of this section.

Section 262. Supervision of public schools vested in superintendent of education.

The supervision of the public schools shall be vested in a Superintendent of Education, whose powers, duties and compensation shall be fixed by law.

Section 263. School funds not to be used for support of sectarian or denominational schools.

No money raised for the support of the public schools shall be appropriated to or used for the support of any sectarian or denominational school.

Section 264. Board of trustees of state university.

The State University shall be under the management and control of a board of trustees, which shall consist of two members from the Congressional district in which the University is located, one from each of the other Congressional districts in the State, the Superintendent of Education, and the Governor, who shall be ex-officio president of the board. The members of the Board of Trustees as now constituted shall hold office until their respective terms expire under existing law, and until their successors shall be elected and confirmed as hereinafter required. Successors to those trustees whose terms expire in nineteen hundred and two shall hold office until nineteen hundred and seven; successors to those trustees whose terms expire in nineteen hundred and four shall hold office until nineteen hundred and eleven; successors to those trustees whose terms expire in nineteen hundred and six shall hold office until nineteen hundred and fifteen; and thereafter their successors shall hold office for a term of twelve years. When the term of any member of such board shall expire, the remaining members of the board shall, by secret ballot, elect his successor; provided, that any trustee so elected shall hold office from the date of his election until his confirmation or rejection by the Senate, and, if confirmed, until the expiration of the term for which he was elected, and until his successor is elected. At every meeting of the Legislature the Superintendent of Education shall certify to the Senate the names of all who shall have been so elected since the last session of the Legislature, and the Senate shall confirm or reject them, as it shall determine is for the best interest of the University. If it reject the names of any members, it shall thereupon elect trustees in the stead of those rejected. In case of a vacancy on said board by death or resignation of a member, or from any cause other than the expiration of his term of office, the board shall elect his successor who shall hold office until the next session of the Legislature. No trustee shall receive any pay or emolument other than his actual expenses incurred in the discharge of his duties as such.

Section 265. Annual payment of interest on funds of University of Alabama; authority to abolish military system at university.

After the ratification of this Constitution there shall be paid out of the treasury of this State at the time and in the manner provided by law, the sum of not less than thirty-six thousand dollars per annum as interest on the funds of the University of Alabama, heretofore covered into the treasury, for the maintenance and support of said institution; provided, that the Legislature shall have the power at any time they deem proper for the best interest of said University to abolish the military system at said institution or reduce the said system to a department of instruction, and that such action on the part of the Legislature shall not cause any diminution of the amount of the annual interest payable out of the treasury for the support and maintenance of said University.

Section 266. Board of trustees of Alabama Polytechnic Institute.

The Alabama Polytechnic Institute, formerly called the Agricultural and Mechanical College, shall be under the management and control of a Board of Trustees, which shall consist of two members from the Congressional district in which the institute is located, and one from each of the other Congressional districts in the State, the State Superintendent of Education and the Governor shall be ex-officio president of the board. The trustees shall be appointed by the Governor, by and with the advice and consent of the Senate, and shall hold office for a term of twelve years, and until their successors shall be appointed and qualified. The board shall be divided into three classes, as nearly equal as may be, so that one-third may be chosen quadriennially. Vacancies occurring in the office of trustees from death or resignation, and the vacancies regularly occurring in the year nineteen hundred and five shall be filled by the Governor, and such appointee shall hold office until the next meeting of the Legislature. Successors to those trustees whose terms expire in nineteen hundred and three shall hold office until nineteen hundred and eleven; successors to those whose terms expire in nineteen hundred and five shall hold office until nineteen hundred and fifteen; and successors to those whose terms expire in nineteen hundred and seven shall hold office until nineteen hundred and nineteen. No trustee shall receive any pay or emolument other than his actual expenses incurred in the discharge of his duties as such.

Section 267. Change of location of Alabama Polytechnic Institute, Alabama Schools for the Deaf and Blind or Alabama Girls Industrial School.

The Legislature shall not have power to change the location of the State University, or the Alabama Polytechnic Institute, or the Alabama school for the Deaf and Blind, or the Alabama Girls' Industrial school, as now established by law, except upon a vote of two-thirds of the Legislature taken by yeas and nays and entered upon the Journals.

Section 268. Provision for taking school census.

The Legislature shall provide for taking a school census by townships and districts throughout the State not oftener than once in two years, and shall provide for the punishment of all persons or officers making false or fraudulent enumerations and returns; provided, the State Superintendent of Education may order and supervise the taking of a new census in any township, district or county, whenever he may have reasonable cause to believe that false or fraudulent returns have been made.

Section 269. Special county school taxes.

The several counties in this State shall have power to levy and collect a special tax not exceeding ten cents on each one hundred dollars of taxable property in such counties, for the support of public schools; provided, that the rate of such tax, the time it is to continue, and the purpose thereof, shall have been first submitted to a vote of the qualified electors of the county, and voted for by three-fifths of those voting at such election; but the rate of such special tax shall not increase the rate of taxation, State and county combined, in any one year, to more than one dollar and twenty-five cents on each one hundred dollars of taxable property; excluding, however, all special county taxes for public buildings, roads, bridges, and the payment of debts existing at the ratification of the Constitution of eighteen hundred and seventy-five. The funds arising from such special school tax shall be so apportioned and paid through the proper school officials to the several schools in the townships and districts in the county that the school terms of the respective schools shall be extended by such supplement as nearly the same length of time as practicable; provided, that this section shall not apply to the cities of Decatur, New Decatur and Cullman.

Section 270. Applicability of article to Mobile county.

The provisions of this article and of any act of the Legislature passed in pursuance thereof to establish, organize and maintain a system of public schools throughout the State, shall apply to Mobile county only so far as to authorize and require the authorities designated by law to draw the portions of the funds to which said county shall be entitled for school purposes and to make reports to the Superintendent of Education as may be prescribed by law; and all special incomes and powers of taxation as now authorized by law for the benefit of public schools in said county shall remain undisturbed until otherwise provided by the Legislature; provided, that separate schools for each race shall always be maintained by said school authorities.

Article XV: Militia

Section 271. Composition of militia; organizing, arming and disciplining militia; naval militia may be organized.

The Legislature shall have power to declare who shall constitute the militia of the State, and to provide for organizing, arming and disciplining the same; and the Legislature may provide for the organization of a State and Naval Militia.

Section 272. Conformance with regulations governing armies of United States.

The Legislature, in providing for the organization, equipment and discipline of the militia, shall conform as nearly as practicable to the regulations for the government of the armies of the United States.

Section 273. Election or appointment of company and regimental officers.

Each company and regiment shall elect its own company and regimental officers; but if any company or regiment shall neglect to elect such officers within the time prescribed by law, they may be appointed by the Governor.

Section 274. Volunteer organizations.

Volunteer organizations of infantry, cavalry, and artillery and naval militia may be formed in such manner and under such restrictions and with such privileges as may be provided by law.

Section 275. Immunity of members from arrest while attending, going to or returning from musters, parades and elections.

The militia and volunteer forces shall, in all cases, except treason, felony and breach of the peace, be privileged from arrest during their attendance at musters, parades and elections and in going to and returning from the same.

Section 276. Appointment and terms of office of general officers; staffs of governor, generals and regimental and battalion commanders.

The Governor shall, with the advice and consent of the Senate, appoint all general officers, whose terms of office shall be four years. The Governor, the generals and regimental and batallion commanders shall appoint their own staffs, as may be provided by law.

Section 277. Safe keeping of arms, ammunition, military records, etc.

The Legislature shall provide for the safe keeping of the arms, ammunition and accoutrements, and military records, banners and relics of the State.

Section 278. Officers and men not entitled to compensation when not in active service.

The officers and men of the militia and volunteer forces shall not be entitled to or receive any pay, rations or emoluments when not in active service.

Article XVI: Oath of Office

Section 279. Required of members of legislature and executive and judicial officers; form; administration.

All members of the Legislature, and all officers, executive and judicial, before they enter upon the execution of the duties of their respective offices, shall take the following oath or affirmation.

"I........., solemnly swear (or affirm, as the case may be), that I will support the Constitution of the United States, and the Constitution of the State of Alabama, so long as I continue a citizen thereof; and that I will faithfully and honestly discharge the duties of the office upon which I am about to enter, to the best of my ability. So help me God."

The oath may be administered by the presiding officer of either House of the Legislature, or by any officer authorized by law to administer an oath.

Article XVII: Miscellaneous Provisions

Section 280. Holding state and federal office at same time; holding two state offices at same time.

No person holding an office of profit under the United States, except postmasters, whose annual salaries do not exceed two hundred dollars, shall during his continuance in such office hold any office of profit under this State; nor, unless otherwise provided in this Constitution, shall any person hold two offices of profit at one and the same time under this State, except Justices of the peace, Constables, Notaries Public, and Commissioners of Deeds.

Section 281. Compensation of civil officers not to be increased or diminished during term for which elected or appointed.

The salary, fees or compensation of any officer holding any civil office of profit under this State or any county or municipality thereof, shall not be increased or diminished during the term for which he shall have been elected or appointed.

Section 282. Duty of legislature to enact laws to effectuate Constitution.

It is made the duty of the Legislature to enact all laws necessary to give effect to the provisions of this Constitution.

Section 283. Validation of certain acts relating to bonded debt of state; governor authorized to act thereunder.

The act of the General Assembly of Alabama entitled "An Act to consolidate and adjust the bonded debt of the State of Alabama," approved February 18th, 1895, and an act amendatory thereof entitled "An Act to amend Section 6 of an act to consolidate and adjust the bonded debt of the State of Alabama, approved February 18th, 1895," which said last named act was approved February 16th, 1899, are hereby made valid, and both of said acts shall have the full force and effect of law, except insofar as they authorize the redemption before maturity of the bonds authorized by said acts to be issued. The Governor is authorized and empowered to act under the same and to carry out all the provisions thereof; provided, that the bonds authorized to be issued by said acts and issued thereunder may be made payable at any time, not exceeding fifty years from the date thereof, and shall not be redeemable until their maturity.

Article XVIII: Mode of Amending the Constitution

Section 284. Manner of proposing amendments; submission of amendments to electors; election on amendments; proclamation of result of election; basis of representation in legislature not to be changed by amendment.

Amendments may be proposed to this Constitution by the Legislature in the manner following: The proposed amendments shall be read in the House in which they originate on three several days, and if upon the third reading three-fifths of all the members elected to that House shall vote in favor thereof, the proposed amendments shall be sent to the other House, in which they shall likewise be read on three several days, and if upon the third reading three-fifths of all the members elected to that House shall vote in favor of the proposed amendments, the Legislature shall order an election by the qualified electors of the State upon such proposed amendments, to be held either at the general election next succeeding the session of the Legislature at which the amendments are proposed or upon another day appointed by the Legislature not less than three months after the final adjournment of the session of the Legislature at which the amendments were proposed. Notice of such election, together with the proposed amendments, shall be given by proclamation of the Governor, which shall be published in every county in such manner as the Legislature shall direct, for at least eight successive weeks next preceding the day appointed for such election. On the day so appointed an election shall be held for the vote of the qualified electors of the State upon the proposed amendments. If such election be held on the day of the general election, the officers of such general election shall open a poll for the vote of the qualified electors upon the proposed amendments; if it be held on a day other than that of a general election, officers for such election shall be appointed; and the election shall be held in all things in accordance with the law governing general elections. In all elections upon such proposed amendments, the votes cast thereat shall be canvassed, tabulated, and returns thereof be made to the Secretary of State, and counted, in the same manner as in elections for Representatives to the Legislature; and if it shall thereupon appear that a majority of the qualified electors who voted at such election upon the proposed amendments voted in favor of the same, such amendments shall be valid to all intents and purposes as parts of this Constitution. The result of such election shall be made known by proclamation of the Governor. Representation in the Legislature shall be based upon population, and such basis of representation shall not be changed by constitutional amendments.

Section 285. Election ballots; affirmative vote of majority of electors voting required for passage.

Upon the ballots used at all elections provided for in Section 284 of this Constitution the substance or subject matter of each proposed amendment shall be so printed that the nature thereof shall be clearly indicated. Following each proposed amendment on the ballot shall be printed the word "Yes" and immediately under that shall be printed the word "No." The choice of the elector shall be indicated by a cross mark made by him or under his direction, opposite the word expressing his desire, and no amendment shall be adopted unless it receives the affirmative vote of a majority of all the qualified electors who vote at such election.

Section 286. Manner of calling convention for purpose of altering or amending Constitution; repeal of act or resolution calling convention; jurisdiction and power of convention not restricted.

No convention shall hereafter be held for the purpose of altering or amending the Constitution of this State, unless after the Legislature by a vote of a majority of all the members elected to each House has passed an act or resolution calling a Convention for such purpose, the question of Convention or No Convention shall be first submitted to a vote of all the qualified electors of the State, and approved by a majority of those voting at such election. No act or resolution of the Legislature calling a convention for the purpose of altering or amending the Constitution of this State, shall be repealed except upon the vote of a majority of all the members elected to each House at the same session at which such act or resolution was passed; provided, nothing herein contained shall be construed as restricting the jurisdiction and power of the convention, when duly assembled in pursuance of this section, to establish such ordinances and to do and perform such things as to the convention may seem necessary or proper for the purpose of altering, revising or amending the existing Constitution.

Section 287. Votes by legislature on proposed amendments or bills or resolutions calling conventions; acts or resolutions proposing amendments or calling conventions not to be submitted to governor for approval.

All votes of the Legislature upon proposed amendments to this Constitution, and upon bills or resolutions calling a Convention for the purpose of altering or amending the Constitution of this State, shall be taken by yeas and nays and entered on the Journals. No act or resolution of the Legislature passed in accordance with the provisions of this article, proposing amendments to this Constitution, or calling a convention for the purpose of altering or amending the Constitution of this State, shall be submitted for the approval of the Governor, but shall be valid without his approval.

Schedule

In order that no injury or inconvenience may arise from the alterations and amendments made by this Constitution to the existing Constitution of this State, and to carry this Constitution into effect, it is hereby ordained and declared:

1. That all laws in force at the ratification of this Constitution and not inconsistent therewith, shall remain in full force until altered or repealed by the Legislature; and all rights, actions, prosecutions, claims and contracts of the State, counties, municipal corporations, individuals or bodies corporate, not inconsistent with this Constitution, shall continue to be valid as if this Constitution had not been ratified.

2. That all bonds executed by or to any officer of this State, all recognizances, obligations and all other instruments executed to this State, or to any subdivision or municipality thereof, before the ratification of this Constitution, and all fines, taxes, penalties and forfeitures due and owing to the State, or any subdivision or municipality thereof; and all writs, suits, prosecutions, claims and causes of action, except as herein otherwise provided, shall continue and remain unaffected by the ratification of this Constitution. All indictments which have been found, or which may hereafter be found, for any crime or offense committed before the ratification of this Constitution, shall be proceeded upon in the same manner as if this Constitution had not been ratified.

3. That all the executive and judicial officers, and all other officers in this State, who were elected at the elections held in this State on the first Monday in August, in the years eighteen hundred and ninety-eight and nineteen hundred, or who have been appointed since that time, and all members of the present General Assembly, and all who may be hereafter elected members of the present

General Assembly, and all other officers holding office at the time of the ratification of this Constitution, shall, except as otherwise provided in this Constitution, continue in office and exercise the duties thereof until their respective terms shall expire, as provided by the Constitution of eighteen hundred and seventy-five, or the laws of this State.

4. This Constitution shall be submitted to the qualified electors of this State for ratification or rejection, as authorized and required by an act of the General Assembly of this State, entitled "An Act to provide for holding a convention to revise and amend the Constitution of this State," approved the eleventh day of December, nineteen hundred; and no elector shall be deprived of his right to vote at the election to be held for such purpose by reason of his not being registered.

5. That instead of the publication as required by the act to provide for holding a convention to revise and amend the Constitution, approved the eleventh day of December, nineteen hundred, the Governor of this State is hereby authorized to take such steps as will give general publicity and circulation to this Constitution in a manner as economical as practicable.

6. The salaries of the Executive and Judicial and all other officers of this State, who may be holding office at the time of the ratification of this Constitution, and the payment of the present members of the General Assembly, shall not be affected by the provisions of this Constitution.

Done by the people of Alabama, through their delegates in convention assembled in the hall of the House of Representatives, at Montgomery, Alabama, this, the third day of September, Anno Domini, nineteen hundred and one.
John B. Knox, President.

Attest: Frank N. Julian, Secretary.

David C. Almon,
W. A. Altman,
John T. Ashcraft,
W. H. Banks,
J. H. Barefield,
W. H. Bartlett,
J. Robert Beavers,
C. P. Beddow,
D. S. Bethune,
Samuel Blackwell,
Burwell Boykin Boone,
Leslie E. Brooks,
Cecil Browne,
Thomas L. Bulger,
John D. Burnett,
John F. Burns (1875-1901),
John A. Byars,
H. W. Cardon,
A. H. Carmichael,
M. S. Carmichael,
G. H. Carnathan,
Davy Crockett Case,
Reuben Chapman,
James Edward Cobb,
W. T. L. Cofer,
Thomas W. Coleman,
E. W. Coleman,
Thomas J. Cornwell,
B. H. Craig,
R. M. Cunningham,
John A. Davis,
Hubert T. Davis,
S. H. Dent,
Ed. deGraffenried ,
Joseph B. Duke,
B. T. Eley,

John C. Eyster,
T. M. Espy,
Charles W. Ferguson,
William C. Fitts,
A. S. Fletcher,
J. M. Foster,
N. H. Freeman,
J. A. Gilmore,
William Franklin Glover,
Edward A. Graham,
Joseph B. Graham,
L. W. Grant,
John W. Grayson,
Leonard F. Greer, Sr.,
Charles H. Greer,
C. L. Haley,
William A. Handley,
Geo. P. Harrison (1875-1901),
J. Thomas Heflin,
John T. Heflin,
Jere C. Henderson,
Evans Hinson,
Patrick W. Hodges,
Oliver R. Hood,
Wilson P. Howell,
Augustin Clayton Howze,
W. B. Inge,
E. C. Jackson,
Samuel C. Jenkins,
John C. Jones,
J. McLean Jones,
Thomas G. Jones,
Richard C. Jones,
James T. Kirk,
W. W. Kirkland,
William N. Knight,
R. B. Kyle,
Emmett W. Ledbetter,

Norville R. Leigh, Jr.,
Lawrence W. Locklin,
Tennent Lomax,
J. Lee Long,
T. L. Long,
Robert J. Lowe,
William T. Lowe,
Gordon Macdonald,
B. F. McMillan,
Lee McMillan,
George H. Malone,
J. T. Martin,
J. C. Maxwell,
Allen H. Merrill,
Charles H. Miller,
Joseph N. Miller,
Milo Moody,
W. O. Mulkey,
Joel D. Murphree (1875-1901),
C. C. NeSmith,
J. D. Norman,
Joseph Norwood,
Wm. C. Oates (1875-1901),
Emmett O'Neal,
John W. O'Neil,
Henry Opp,
Rufus A. O'Rear,
Dabney Palmer,
George H. Parker,
John H. Parker, Sr.,
James P. Pearce,
Erle Pettus,
E. A. Phillips,
Harry Pillans,
P. H. Pitts,
John H. Porter,
John Franklin Proctor,
Henry Fontaine Reese (Dallas),

N. P. Renfro,
R. J. Reynolds,
J. J. Robinson,
C. P. Rogers, Sr.,
John Aduston Rogers of Sumter County, Ala.
Wm. Hodges Samford,
W. T. Sanders,
John William Augustine Sanford,
George A. Searcy,
Henry C. Selheimer,
James O. Sentell,
J. B. Sloan, Jr.,
Gregory L. Smith,
Mac. A. Smith,
Morgan M. Smith,
M. Sollie,
George A. Sorrell,
Napoleon B. Spears,
Robert E. Spragins,
J. H. Stewart,
W. H. Tayloe,
J. F. Thompson,
Watkins M. Vaughan,
Boswell deGraffenried Waddell,
Richard W. Walker

www.ingramcontent.com/pod-product-compliance
Lightning Source LLC
Chambersburg PA
CBHW052258220526
45471CB00001B/387